UNIVERSITY OF NORTH CAROLINA
STUDIES IN THE ROMANCE LANGUAGES AND LITERATURES
Number 52

THE PHONOLOGICAL HISTORY OF VEGLIOTE

THE PHONOLOGICAL HISTORY OF VEGLIOTE

BY

ROGER L. HADLICH

CHAPEL HILL

THE UNIVERSITY OF NORTH CAROLINA PRESS

DEPÓSITO LEGAL: V. 1.237 - 1965

ARTES GRÁFICAS SOLER, S. A. — VALENCIA — 1965

ACKNOWLEDGEMENTS

This study was originally offered and accepted as partial fulfillment of the requirements for the degree of Doctor of Philosophy in Romance Languages and Literatures at the University of Michigan in June, 1961. I have made a few changes in the original work to take into account facts which have come to my attention since that time.

The assistance of Robert L. Politzer in the original suggestion of the subject and in the continued development of the research is gratefully acknowledged, along with the aid of the other members of the doctoral committee: O. L. Chavarría-Aguilar, Charles W. Kreidler, Herbert Penzl, and Ernst Pulgram. I wish to thank Charles W. Bidwell of the University of Pittsburgh and Žarko Muljačić of the University of Zadar for their careful reading of the original manuscript and for their helpful suggestions. For any deficiencies remaining in the work, however, the responsibility is entirely my own.

I am grateful to the Hull Memorial Publication Fund of Cornell University for partial subvention of the cost of publication.

In the last analysis, however, the most profound debt is owed to the man whose untiring scholarship and zeal produced the work which is fundamental to this work and to all studies of Dalmatian Romance: Matteo G. Bartoli.

ROGER L. HADLICH
Cornell University, 1963.

TRANSCRIPTION

č	pre-palatal voiceless affricate: /čit/ = Eng. *cheat*.
ǧ	pre-palatal voiced affricate: /ǧəmp/ = Eng. *jump*.
ç	alveolar voiceless affricate: /çio/ = Ital. *zio*.
ʒ	alveolar voiced affricate: /ʒona/ = Ital. *zona*.
j	palatal voiced semi-vowel or semi-consonant: /jok/ = Eng. *yoke*.
w	bilabial voiced semi-vowel or semi-consonant: /wik/ = Eng. *week*.
ŋ	velar voiced nasal continuant: /səŋ/ = Eng. *sung*.
r	alveolar voiced flap: /tres/ = Span. *tres*.
r̥	syllabic *r*: [kr̥k] = *Krk*, Serbo-Croatian name for the island of Veglia.
ü	high palatal or front rounded vowel: /bü/ = French. *but*.
ï	high back unrounded vowel: /romïnə/ = Rum. *Romîna*.
ɨ	high central unrounded vowel: /sɨn/ = Russ. *syn*.
ə	mid central unrounded vowel: /pən/ = Eng. *pun*.
æ	low front vowel: /bæt/ = Eng. *bat*.
ɛ	low mid front vowel: /bɛt/ = Eng. *bet*.
ɔ	low back vowel: /bɔt/ = Eng. *bought*.
i̯ u̯	semi-vocalic [i] and [u]: These symbols are used only in Appendix B, where reference is necessary to specific graphs in source material.
ʼ	The apostrophe is used to indicate palatal articulation: /anʼo/ = Span. *año*.
:	vowel or consonant length.
[ ]	indicate that the enclosed transcription is phonetic.
/ /	indicate that the enclosed transcription is phonemic.
>	"becomes".
=	"corresponds to".

ABBREVIATIONS

Cent. Ital.	Central Italian.
C. L.	Classical Latin.
Eng.	English.
Ital.	Italian.
Lat.	Latin: used without specific reference to time or place spoken.
Mod. Vegl.	Modern Vegliote: the language of the nineteenth century materials.
No. Ital.	Northern Italian.
OCS.	Old Church Slavonic.
Old. Vegl.	Old Vegliote: the language subsequent to the beginning of PSCr. influence, but before the language of the modern materials.
PSCr.	Proto-Serbo-Croatian: The reconstructed earliest ancestor in Dalmatia of Mod. SCr.
RRom.	Raeto-Romance.
Rum.	Rumanian.
Russ.	Russian.
Sard.	Sardinian.
SCr.	Serbo-Croatian.
So. Ital.	Southern Italian.
Span.	Spanish.
Vegl.	Vegliote.
Vegl. Lat.	Vegliote Latin: the reconstructed dialect of Latin presumably spoken on the island of Veglia before the influence of PSCr.
Ven.	Venetian.

TABLE OF CONTENTS

	Pages
ACKNOWLEDGEMENTS ...	7
TRANSCRIPTION ...	9
ABBREVIATIONS ...	11

PART ONE

INTRODUCTION

CHAPTER	I.	OBJECTIVES ...	17
—	II.	THE STATUS OF RESEARCH ON VEGLIOTE ...	19
—	III.	METHODS ...	22

      A. Synchronic analysis.
      B. Linguistic reconstruction.
      C. Contrastive analysis.
      D. Relative chronology.
      E. Diachronic phonemics.

| — | IV. | EVIDENCE ... | 29 |
| — | V. | EXTERNAL HISTORY ... | 32 |

PART TWO

THE HISTORY OF VEGLIOTE

		PREFATORY NOTE ...	37
—	VI.	PERIOD ONE: THE LATIN OF VEGLIA ...	39
—	VII.	PERIOD TWO: THE EARLIEST SERBO-CROATIAN INFLUENCE.	42

      A. The early Serbo-Croatian phonemic system.
      B. The effect on the Latin of Veglia.

| — | VIII. | PERIOD THREE: LATER SERBO-CROATIAN CHANGES AND THEIR REFLECTION IN VEGLIOTE ... | 46 |

      A. Changes in Serbo-Croatian in Period Three.
      B. The Effects on Vegliote.

Pages

CHAPTER IX. PERIOD FOUR. THE CHANGES WHICH PRODUCED MODERN
VEGLIOTE 49
    A. Serbo-Croatian changes in Period Four.
    B. Venetian.
    C. Vegliote developments in Period Four.
    D. Consonantal changes in Period Four.

PART THREE

APPENDICES

APPENDIX A. PHONEMIC ANALYSIS OF MODERN VEGLIOTE 57
APPENDIX B. LATIN-VEGLIOTE SOUND CORRESPONDENCES 71
APPENDIX C. CHART OF THE VOWEL HISTORY OF VEGLIOTE, SERBO-
CROATIAN, AND VENETIAN 77
APPENDIX D. DISCUSSION OF SELECTED PROBLEMS 79
    A. C.L. /a/.
    B. C.L. /a/, /ĕ/ and /ŏ/.
    C. C.L. /ō/ and /ŭ/.
    D. The Development of the groups /kt/, /ks/,
       /pt/, and /ps/.
    E. East or West?
BIBLIOGRAPHY 89

PART ONE

INTRODUCTION

CHAPTER ONE

OBJECTIVES

This is a study of the phonology of the Romance language called Vegliote,[1] spoken until 1899 on the island of Veglia, now called Krk, which is located in the Quarnaro Gulf off the coast of Yugoslavia. The study represents an attempt to apply the techniques of structural linguistics to the entire phonological history of one language.[2]

The purpose of the study is two-fold: to present a clear picture of the structural history of Vegl., and to illustrate the applicability of structural linguistics to a diachronic study of many stages.

In Part One, the background for the analysis is outlined. Discussed in particular are the status of research on Vegl.; the methods used in studying the history of Vegl.; the problem of evidence of linguistic change; and the external history of Vegl.

Part Two is the core of the dissertation. It comprises a presentation of the results of the study. In it, the history of the Vegl. sound system is outlined and the factors which influenced the changes in the language are discussed. Of importance are the

---

[1] The speakers of the language called it "Veklisun". "Veglioto" was used by Bartoli, and it occurs in all subsequent works in some variation of this form, although "Vegliotic" is also used in publications in English.

[2] Two other works have been written on structural history, one on French and one on Spanish, which embrace comparable spans of time. Haudricourt—Juilland, 1949; and Alarcos Llorach, 1954, 179-226. The work by Haudricourt and Juilland does not cover all of the development of French from Latin, but the problems treated are some of the most fundamental problems in the linguistic history of French. Alarcos Llorach works with entire phonological history of Spanish.

problem of the variety of Latin spoken in Veglia, the effect of PSCr. on that Latin, and the later increasing influence of Venetian.

Part Three, the appendices, is peripheral to the core in that it includes information which, although frequently fundamental to the analysis, is not of crucial importance to the historical outline. The appendices represent amplifications of certain features of the history. The information contained in the appendices is excluded from Part Two so as to avoid unnecessarily complicated explanation which would tend to obscure the over-all patterning of the history.

Appendix A is a phonemic analysis of Mod. Vegl. Appendix B gives the sound correspondences between Latin and Mod. Vegl., with examples. Appendix C is a chart illustrating the vowel changes discussed in Part Two. Appendix D contains a more detailed discussion of certain features of the phonological history, including, for example, certain fundamental points on which the present work shows previous research to have been inadequate or in error.

Chapter Two

THE STATUS OF RESEARCH ON VEGLIOTE

In the 1890's, with only one speaker of Vegl. remaining, Matteo G. Bartoli, the Italian linguist, became aware of the impending extinction of the language and he commenced collecting all available materials, published and unpublished, on Vegl. In addition, he was able to spend a considerable amount of time with the last speaker of Vegl., and he succeeded in recording in phonetic script a large sample of the informant's speech.[1]

Bartoli worked on his materials for about nine years, during which time he collected a great deal of information on the history and geography of Dalmatia, and he pursued every possible linguistic reference to Dalmatian, including such things as a hand-written copy book containing notes on Vegl. made by a curious young man some years previously. In 1906 Bartoli published his research in a two volume work entitled *Das Dalmatische*.[2]

---

[1] BARTOLI, 1906, II, 7-80.

[2] Although the work purports to deal with Dalmatian Romance, by far the greatest mass of material is that for Vegl., the data for the rest of Dalmatia being at best scanty. I have concentrated my attention on the material gathered by Bartoli from the informant. The reason for working primarily with this material is that the most effective phonemic analysis relies on the consideration of a corpus of phonetic data large enough to permit observation and analyses of patterning. Although the informant is no longer available for checking inconsistencies, Bartoli's phonetic transcription provides an adequate body of material to afford a structural analysis which counteracts these inconsistencies.

The materials on the rest of Dalmatia, in addition to being quite scarce, represent cullings from texts from other linguistic studies, and from various informants. The restriction to Vegl. adds reliability to the analysis, but it permits of no broad generalizations regarding Dalmatian or Balkan Romance.

The work is a repository of everything that might be considered related to Vegl. and Dalmatia. The author included detailed geographical, historical, and ethnological studies; a full description of all materials, and his methods of obtaining them; a complete reproduction of all previously published texts; maps, word lists, and pictures. Most important to my analysis is Bartoli's description of phonology, morphology, and lexicon, and the comparison of Vegl. with other Romance languages.

Bartoli's phonological analysis is based on the nineteenth century tradition, in which the history of a given sound was discussed without much consideration of systematic patterning, and without the rigorous application of structural methods. The result of his analysis is a set of phonetic sound correspondences between C. L. and Vegl. My own analysis was started on the assumption that the re-examination of the same materials in the light of developments in linguistic theory since 1906 could offer new insights into the history of Vegl.

Immediately following the publication of Bartoli's work, a number of reviews appeared in print, most of which were quite complimentary.[3] Most interesting of the reviews is that by Clemente Merlo (1907). In this review, in addition to disapproving of Bartoli's methodology ("anzitutto poca prezisione, una grande incertezza...", 473), and disagreeing with a large number of conclusions regarding sound correspondences and etymologies, Merlo criticizes at great length Bartoli's conclusion that Vegl. is closely related to So. Ital. dialects. He finally cites Ascoli (1873), who believed that Ladin, Ven., and Vegl. are very closely related.

Ensuing from this first review by Merlo is a long series of criticisms, counter-remarks, proofs, and reproofs, which extended until 1954.[4] The essence of the controversy, which became very personal and amazingly bitter, was whether Vegl. was more closely related to the RRom. or to the So. Ital. dialects. Although Bartoli con-

---

[3] BARLOLI (1910, 457, n. 6) cites as complimentary reviews by BESZARD, 1908; GARTNER, 1907; JUD, 1909; PARODI, 1907; PUŞCARIU, 1907; and ZAUNER, 1907.

[4] BARTOLI, 1908; MERLO, 1910; BARTOLI, 1910; MERLO, 1924; BARTOLI, 1926; MERLO, 1929, and 1954.

ceded certain points, he never abandoned his contention that Vegl. was an East Romance language, hence closer to So. Ital.

The bibliography I have appended indicates the extent of my indebtedness to other·scholars who have worked on Vegl. and related topics. Certain of these scholars, however, deserve special mention because their work has proved to be particularly useful.

Bartoli's *Das Dalmatische* referred to above is the most extensive and the most important treatment of Vegl. From it I have extracted the majority of my data, and it has proved a source of constant reference for all phases of the study.

Peter Skok has produced many important contributions to the study of the languages of the Balkan peninsula. All of those works cited in the bibliography must be considered basic to the study of Vegl.

John V. Elmendorf's etymological dictionary of Vegl. was of frequent assistance as a reference work.

The most recent work on Vegl. is that of Petar Guberina. His study of the history of the Vegl. vowels is discussed below, 80-82.

Alwin Kuhn's *Romanische Philologie* (I, 142-156) contains the best discussion of the status of research on Vegl.

CHAPTER THREE

METHODS

I understand the term "method" in reference to linguistics to denote a particular manner in which a set of linguistic data is used. Handling of linguistic data can be broadly divided into two categories: internal and external. All of the traditional techniques of description (e.g., studies in phonology, morphology, syntax, lexicography, etc.) result from the internal examination of the data. Linguistic data from one language may also be considered externally, i.e., in relation to information outside that language. Such consideration gives rise to studies in linguistic geography, comparative reconstruction, bilingual studies, etc.

It has become increasingly evident to me that in large scale studies where an entire language or dialect is examined over a period of centuries, the espousal of one particular method to the exclusion of others leads to conclusions based on inadequate information and hence to misrepresentation. I believe that, in the historical analysis of a language, all applicable techniques must be utilized, and the final description must take all findings into account, leaving no residue.

The following is a discussion of the specific application of several methods to the historical analysis of Vegl.

A. *Synchronic analysis.*

The first attack on the problem of Vegl. was the phonemic analysis of the phonetic corpus for Mod. Vegl. published by Bartoli. The results of the analysis are presented in Appendix A.

The phonemic analysis of Mod. Vegl. resulted in the systematic organization of the raw data and served as a frame of reference for the discussion of earlier stages of the language. Mod. Vegl. provides the only thoroughly attested stage of Vegl., hence this analysis is the keystone in the whole study.

Structural analysis was also used at several stages of the history. No reconstructed phoneme or phonemic change was described without consideration of its relation to the total system.

B. *Linguistic reconstruction.*

After the phonemic analysis of Mod. Vegl. it was possible to express the lexicon in terms of phonemes, thereby providing the material upon which the reconstruction of the earlier stages of Vegl. was based.

The reconstruction of earlier forms of Vegl. was accomplished primarily by means of comparative techniques, and those of internal reconstruction. The comparative method, as outlined, for example, by Bloomfield, starts with two or more languages which are assumed to be later forms of an earlier single language. The objective of the comparative method is normally the reconstruction of the parent language. It was not the purpose of this study to reconstruct Latin, but since earlier forms of Vegl. were of primary importance, the application of comparative techniques permitted the forming of hypotheses for those earlier stages which could be tested by using other analytical methods.

The first comparative procedure is to establish patterns of regularity between the languages being compared. The patterns are abstracted from a long list of cognate words. For example, it was found that words containing /i/ in the large majority of Romance languages consistently contained either /e/ or /aj/ in Mod. Vegl.

Ital.	Span.	French	Rum.	Vegl.
filo	hilo	fil	fir	fajl
prima	prima	prime	prima	prajma
mille	mil	mille	mie	mel
ricco	rico	riche	——	rek

It was discovered that the dual representation of /i/ in Vegl. could be accounted for by assuming the bifurcation of an earlier Vegl. phoneme, the later Vegl. result dependent on whether the phoneme had been followd by one consonant or more than one. Since the correspondence between /i/ in most Romance languages and the /e/ and /aj/ in Vegl. was regular, the postulation was indicated that those words containing /e/ and /aj/ developed from words which, at least at one stage in the history of Vegl., contained /i/.

Following a series of similar comparisons, it was possible to reconstruct earlier versions of all the Mod. Vegl. phonemes. Subsequent application of information obtained from other sources (history, bilingual contact with SCr., linguistic geography, etc.) served to refine the assumptions made about the earlier stages of Vegl.

The comparative method was also used in this study in the reconstruction of PSCr. Since the external history of Veglia shows intimate and continued contact between Vegl. and SCr., the history of SCr. was of great interest. The data used for the reconstruction of PSCr. were taken primarily from OCS., which is attested from the ninth century on, and from Mod. SCr.

C. *Contrastive analysis.*

In *Languages in Contact* (14-29), Uriel Weinreich analyzes in great detail the processes involved in the speaking of a second language, and the resultant phonic interference (or "foreign accent") caused by the native language structure. He also discusses the diffusion of these interference phenomena. Fundamental to this discussion of diffusion and to my study is the assumption that, through the medium of bilingual speakers, subphonemic characteristics can be transferred from one language to another, given suitable structural and cultural conditions.[1]

Following Weinreich's reasoning, it is possible to predict in what ways the phenomenon of interference might effect the speech pro-

---

[1] Hoenigswald (1960, 73) extends this concept to suggest that *all* language change may be the result of subdialectal borrowing. According to Swadesh (1951, 59) the importance of the bilingual in language change was stressed by Sapir, and it goes back to the work of Boas.

duction of a speaker of a second language. By extension of the same reasoning, it is possible at least to suggest what structural features might be transferable from one language to another, if two languages come into close contact.

The method by which linguistic interference is predicted on the synchronic level is called contrastive analysis. The procedure is the separate phonemic analysis of the two languages in contact, and the comparison of these two analyses in order to determine at what points the two systems are parallel, and at what points interference in second language production will tend to occur.

Weinreich established four basic types of phonic interference: [2]

1. Under-differentiation of phonemes, where two phonemes in the secondary system are confused because they are not distinguished in the primary language. 2. Over-differentiation of phonemes, where distinctions are made in the secondary system although they are not required, owing to a distinction in the primary. 3. Reinterpretation of distinctions, where the bilingual distinguishes phonemes in the secondary system by means of features which are redundant in that system, but which are significant in the primary system. 4. Phone substitution, where the bilingual uses a phoneme of the primary language as if it were identical to a phoneme in the second language. Interference of this last type takes place when the primary phoneme used differs in pronunciation from the secondary phoneme. The transfer of this difference to the second language produces the foreign accent.

Although these terms were established primarily in reference to synchronic interference, they apply also to the structural effect of one language on another in their historical development, because this external influence is viewed as the transfer to the second language of those features arising from interference in the speech of bilinguals. [3]

For the study on Vegl., all historical and linguistic indications are that there had been strong bilingual influence of SCr. and Ven. on Vegl. As a result, one of the most important operations was the comparison of the phonemic systems of the three languages at

---

[2] 1953, 18-19.
[3] Cf. WEINREICH, 1953, 23-24, *Diffusion of phonic interference phonomena*.

several crucial historical stages in order to describe the possible influences on Vegl.

D. *Relative chronology.*

Since the primary objective of this study involved the structural description of unattested phonemic changes, a great deal of attention was necessarily given to chronological sequence of the many changes. Interest in relative chronology in historical description is nothing new. It can be seen in the work of Meyer-Lübke,[4] Richter,[5] Menéndez-Pidal,[6] and many others. Recent work by G. Straka treats relative chronology as a method of analysis.[7]

The logic of relative chronology may be illustrated as follows: if one observes a linguistic change x, which took place while condition A existed in the language, and a change y which took place after condition A was lost from the language, then x is necessarily prior to y. In essence a simple operation, such relations become extremely complex as the number of conditions involved increases. The following is offered as an example of how certain developments in the history of Vegl. have been related to the beginning of PSCr. influence, hence before or after the seventh century: Mod. Vegl. shows that earlier /a/ and /ɔ/ merged. However, since they have the same Mod. Vegl. results in both free and blocked syllable, this merger must have taken place before the phonemic split of vowels that was dependent on the type of syllable (free or blocked) in which they occurred.[8] Comparative criteria and contrastive analysis determine the placement of the merger or /a/ and /ɔ/ after the beginning of PSCr. influence on Vegl. Therefore, vowel differentiation must have occurred after the beginning of PSCr. influence. In a like manner, Lat. long consonants, which have simplified in Mod. Vegl.,

---

[4] 1908, 266-267.
[5] 1934.
[6] 1952, 171-174.
[7] 1956.
[8] "Free syllable" refers to a syllable ending in a vowel, "blocked syllable" to one ending in a consonant. The phonemic split of vowels dependent on the type of syllable is referred to hereafter as "vowel differentiation". Cf. "Vokaldifferenzierung" in Weinrich, 1959, Ch. 8.

were still long at the time vowel differentiation took place, since they had the effect of blocking the preceding syllable. Therefore the loss of phonemic consonant length must have taken place contemporaneously with, or after, vowel differentiation, and therefore after the influence of PSCr. on Vegl. began.

Such chains of chronological relation were frequent in the analysis of the history of Vegl., so that relative chronology, usually supplemented or supported by information gleaned from other sources, was an extremely important factor in my analysis.

E. *Diachronic phonemics.*

I use the term diachronic phonemics in the broadest possible sense: the application to linguistic history of the phonemic principle, and of the concept that language change must always be considered in relation to the linguistic system. Unfortunately, diachronic phonemics has recently fallen into some disrepute,[9] largely, I feel, because critics have focused their attention on individual theories or on individual features of the techniques, to the detriment of the whole.

It would be well, in view of the recent criticism, to summarize here the relation between my methods of analysis and some of the more widely discussed principles of diachronic phonemics.

Current theory holds that the relative importance to communication of a phonemic opposition (i.e., the functional load of that opposition) has an influence on whether or not the opposition is lost or preserved in the course of history.[10] There was no possibility of discussing the effect or functional load on the specific changes in Vegl. because of the lack of earlier stages sufficiently well attested to permit computations.

No indication was discovered that the tendency toward linguistic symmetry[11] affected any Vegl. change. On the contrary, external influences were often found to have the effect of breaking a

---

[9] See especially VIDOS, 1959, 135-163; COSERIU, 1958, Ch. VI and TOGEBY, 1960, 401-413.
[10] MARTINET, 1955, 54-58.
[11] *Ibid.,* Ch. IV.

symmetrical pattern. However, subsequent internal adjustments to changes in the system induced by foreign influence frequently resulted in a symmetrical system in Vegl.

There is no evidence that the so-called asymmetry of the speech organs [12] had any effect whatsoever on the phonological changes in Vegl.

On the other hand, chain reactions [13] of phonemic changes are clearly illustrated in the history of Vegl. The phonemic vowel shifts of Vegl. in the final period of its development (see below, 51) provide some classical examples of chain reactions.

Although I have just pointed out that a number of diachronic phonemic theories had no application in my analysis of Vegl., it has not been my intention to criticize these theories. The examples offer further underscoring of the point that in using the methods of diachronic phonemics I employ not a series of separate principles, but rather the comprehensive attitude of structural analysis, which is as applicable to linguistic history as it is to synchronic description.

A final note on the relation between diachronic phonemics and the other four methods discussed (22-27, above): I have used the term diachronic phonemics and discussed it as if it were a method of handling data separate from linguistic geography, comparative reconstruction, contrastive analysis, etc. In fact, it is not. In my analysis, structural criteria were always considered whenever dealing with Vegl. from any of the other methodological points of view, and invariably insights were gained which would have been unavailable in a non-structural approach. Structural analysis in historical linguistics is not a school of thought which may be espoused or rejected according to the taste of the linguist, but a vigorous and productive addition to linguistic techniques which must be taken into consideration.

---

[12] *Ibid.*, 95-96.
[13] *Ibid.*, 56-63.

CHAPTER FOUR

EVIDENCE

Evidence for phonemic change has been classified and typed by Herbert Penzl.[1] He describes five general types of evidence: orthographic, orthoëpic, metrical, comparative, and contact evidence. Of these five types, two are unavailable for Vegl. orthoëpic, which is produced when grammarians write about a language, and metrical evidence, found in the rime and meter of poetry. The three types of evidence available were useful in varying degrees.

1. Orthographic evidence of earlier stages of Vegl. consist of occasional items, usually place names or names of people, found in Latin or Italianizing texts, and which reflect some feature of Vegl. phonology.[2] Note that, excepting the modern phonetic corpus of Bartoli's work and a few written documents from the modern period, no extended text written in Vegl. is extant. The sporadic character of the historical attestations places certain restrictions on the conclusions that may be drawn from this orthographic evidence. Because of the nature of writing and its relation to language, the positive evidence that a given sound change has taken place can be reliable proof, but the lack of evidence for change is dubious proof of anything. This is all the more true in cases like Vegl. where historical documents do not contain enough data to reflect the whole system of the language at any given point except the present. Thus orthopraphic evidence can be used only to establish relative

---

[1] 1957.
[2] The best studies of these documents are found in BARTOLI, *Das Dalmatische*, and SKOK, *Studi toponomastici*...

chronology and rough dating of phonological changes in the history of Vegl.

2. Comparative evidence, on the other hand, was especially helpful for the study of Vegl. Penzl subdivides comparative evidence into a number of types, most of which I have utilized.

Syncomparative evidence is based on data obtained by the comparison of two languages. In particular, cognate words in Vegl. and in dialects of Central and Northern Italy were used in the reconstruction of the variety of Latin spoken in Veglia prior to the sixth century. (Se above, 23-24, for an example of the use of syncomparative evidence.)

Diacomparative evidence, found in two different stages of the same language, excepting the individual attestations mentioned above was unavailable for Vegl. However, such evidence was available for the dialects of Northern Italy, which, although it offered no proof for Vegl., aided in the formation of hypotheses for Vegl. which could be checked against other data. An example is the textual attestation that Latin long consonants were intact in the eighth century in Northern Italy.[3] This evidence led to the hypothesis that long consonants existed in Vegl. Lat. in the sixth century. The hypothesis was sustained by comparison with the effect of PSCr. on Vegl. Lat.

Internal comparison of elements within one language can reveal certain patterning which aids in clarifying otherwise obscure developments in the history of the language. For example, the only reliable Vegl. words containing the reflex of Lat. /kt/ indicate /t/ as its normal development (App. D, 84-85). However, evidence of the preservation of many other clusters (e.g., /pt/, /ps/) gives weight to the assumption that Lat. /kt/ was preserved in Vegl., and that the examples with /t/ are to be accounted for by influence of Ven., either as loan words, or by the interference of Ven. in the informant's production of Vegl.

Although internal comparison was employed for Vegl. for each reconstructed stage, and although each system was examined for internal continuity, there is little attestation of Vegl. at any of these stages.

---

[3] POLITZER, 1953, 12-13.

Areal distribution of phonic features may be considered comparative evidence. Information gained from evidence of this type was very helpful to me in postulating certain phonological features of Vegl. Lat. For example, the geographical distribution of [ej] in reflexes of C.L. /ē/ in a continuous area from Raetia and Northern Italy through Istria, along with its probable development in these areas prior to the seventh century led to the assumption that the reflex of C.L. /ē/ was pronounced [ej] also on the island of Veglia, which is immediately adjacent to the above area. Since the Mod. Vegl. reflex for C.L. /ē/ is /aj/, this assumption seemed well supported. Another example is the distribution of /ü/ in Northern Italy. In the history of Vegl., words with the Vegl. equivalent of C.L. /ū/ had a stage with a palatal articulation [ü]. However, since the modern distribution of /ü/ in Northern Italy shows that it grows less frequent toward the East, and does not occur in Friulian, Ven., or Istrian, the Vegl. /ü/ cannot have been brought to Veglia as a result of a phonological wave. The implication is that Vegl. /ü/ was not directly associated with the No. Ital. /ü/, and other causes must be sought for its development.

Neo-comparative evidence as described by Penzl is found in a modern language and it shows the completion of phonemic shifts, mergers and splits. It is in the phonetic corpus of Mod. Vegl. that the preponderance of data is contained, and thus the historical study of Vegl. relies to a large degree on neo-comparative evidence.

3. The fifth of the types of evidence described by Penzl is that resulting from the contact of two languages. For this, loan words constitute the primary source.[4] I have utilized Lat. loan words in SCr., and to a restricted degree, SCr. loan words in Vegl. offer some assistance. An example of the former is the existence in SCr. of Lat. loan words containing /k/ before former Lat. /i/ or /e/, some of which still maintain a stop articulation in Mod. SCr., e.g. C.L. *cepulla* = SCr. /kapula/. The high frequency of the borrowing and the type of word borrowed permit the discounting of a learned influence in these loan words. The loans, then, establish that in Dalmatian Latin the /k/ continued to be articulated as a stop until after the arrival of the Slavic-speaking migrants.

---

[4] BIDWELL has done an interesting study on Lat. loans in SCr. (1961).

CHAPTER FIVE

EXTERNAL HISTORY

Latin was first brought to Dalmatia, and presumably to nearby Veglia, in the second century, B.C. Prior to the ascendancy of Roman power in the area, Dalmatia was inhabited by peoples called Illyrians, about whom little enough is known,[1] and by speakers of Greek who had come into the area as a result of Greek commercial enterprise in the whole Mediterranean area. By the last Dalmatian-Pannonic War (9 B.C.), Rome's control over the area was complete, and it remained so at least until the first Gothic invasions in A. D. 395. It can be said that Dalmatia and the coastal islands were Roman until the Slavic invaders, from the early seventh century on, wrested Dalmatia from Rome. These Slavic-speaking invaders gradually pushed the former inhabitants toward the coastal islands. By the middle of the seventh century the Latin-speaking inhabitants of Dalmatia were concentrated in a few small areas.

From the seventh century until the beginning of the eleventh century, when the first Venetian settlers began arriving in the area, SCr. was the primary linguistic influence. Politically, Dalmatia was under the nominal control of Byzantium, and there must have been a certain amount of Byzantine cultural influence through trade and through the church; but Greek linguistic influence in Mod. Vegl. is restricted to a few lexical items.

The bishop and the prior of Veglia first swore allegiance to Venice under Pietro Orseolo in 998, but shortly thereafter, Veglia was again subjected to the kings of Croatia. Thence Veglia embarked

---

[1] PULGRAM, 1958, 168-170.

on a period of changing sovereignty variously under the Magyars, the Croatians and the Venetians until 1480 when Venice established control for a period not to end until 1796. The period from about 1000 to 1480, mottled though it may appear by frequent changes of sovereignty, had one continuing feature: The Frankapan counts. This family, apparently of Venetian origin, gained local control of the countship of Veglia, and except for a period of a few years, they stayed in power on the island regardless of who commanded their allegiance until Giovanni (Zuane) was forced to relinquish all claims in 1480. (During the period after 1358 when Veglia became a part of the Hungarian domain, the Frankapan family not only retained the countship of Veglia, but their seat on the Grand Council of Venice, as well.) [2]

As for the linguistic influence of Venetian during the early period, Skok is of the opinion that it was brought to the Dalmatian islands by Venetian fisherman as early as the period between the ninth and the eleventh centuries, well before the political star of Venice had reached its zenith. Though SCr. was constantly present from the seventh century on, Ven. as well began to be an influence on Vegl. fairly soon after the turn of the millenium. Ven. and SCr. were both spoken on Veglia at the end of the nineteenth century.

The history of Veglia subsequent to 1796 offers little of interest linguistically, although politically, change was again the order. In 1797 it became a part of the Austrian Empire, which it remained, except for a brief period under Napoleon, until the present century, when Austria lost this territory as a result of World War I. In 1924, after a few years of dispute between Italy and Yugoslavia over control of Istria, Fiume, and the coastal islands, Veglia became a part of Yugoslavia. During the Second World War, Veglia was occupied by Italy, 1941-43, and by Germany, 1943-45.

---

[2] The best summary I have found of the history of Veglia, and of Dalmatia, is in JACKSON, 1887. See especially Vol. I, Chap. 1, and Vol. III, Chap. 26.

PART TWO

THE HISTORY OF VEGLIOTE

PREFATORY NOTE

In a synchronic analysis of the language of an informant, the analyst works simultaneously with materials from many structural levels of the language, but his final description is presented in terms of separate levels (i.e., phonemic, morphemic, syntactic). Similarly, the analysis of the history of Vegl. was accompanied by consideration of criteria from different periods of time, and by utilization of information from all of the sources indicated in Part One, Chapters Two and Three. But the results of the analysis are presented, for the sake of clarity, in chronological sequence.

In the interests of simplicity, detailed discussion of individual points has been severely restricted. Although each point is backed by indirect evidence from several sources, the ultimate defense of any one point must be its cohesiveness with the whole description.

This study purports to answer questions on how Vegl. developed, and in some cases, why. It is presented as *an* answer to these questions. That it cannot be *the* answer follows from the lack of evidence for the earlier stages of the language. But since all available data and all applicable analytic techniques were carefully employed, it represents, I believe, the best answer attainable.

The historical description is divided into four periods of development. In Chapter VI (Period One) the period prior to the beginning of PSCr. influence is presented. It contains in outline the reconstruction of the Vegl. Lat. sound system. In Chapter VII (Period Two) the PSCr. phonemic system is presented, and the effects of this language on Vegl. Lat. are suggested. The discussion in Chapter VIII (Period Three) focuses on subsequent changes in PSCr. and their reflection in Vegl. The changes which take place in

Period Four (Chapter IX), related to the influence of both Ven. and SCr., produce the Mod. Vegl. phonemic system.

Since there is little documentation for the exact dating of these periods, I avoid attaching presumed dates for the periods. However, I mention indirect evidence giving general chronological indications whenever it is available.

CHAPTER SIX

PERIOD ONE:
THE LATIN OF VEGLIA

This chapter comprises a description of the phonemic system of the Latin spoken on the island of Veglia immediately prior to the Slavic invasions. The beginning of PSCr. influence in the seventh century serves as a *terminus ante quem* and permits the description of traits in Vegl. Lat. existing prior to this influence. The system was obtained primarily by internal reconstruction in Mod. Vegl., but comparative evidence was also utilized. The details of the reconstruction process are not presented here since they are given in Chapters VII-IX.

A. *Vowels.*

Reconstruction reveals that the variety of Latin spoken in Veglia in this period had seven vowel phonemes: /i e ɛ a ɔ o u/.[1] Although there are no modern equivalents for the Lat. semi-vowel /j/ and only a few for /w/, these two phonemes were necessarily part of this system, since they have an umlaut effect which must have taken place after this first period: e.g., Lat. *-ariu* > Mod. Vegl. -/ir/.[2]

---

[1] Schemas representing this and following stages are reproduced in the fold-out chart of Appendix C. Subsequent description will follow this chart closely.

[2] If the umlaut effect had taken place prior to PSCr. influence and the /i/ had dropped, the resultant /i/ (< /a/ + — /i/) would have followed the later development for Vegl. Lat. /i/ (> Mod. Vegl. /aj/).

Internal reconstruction permits the description of phonetic values of these phonemes in certain positions. By the time of the Slavic migrations all vowels of this system had a long variant in free syllable and a short variant in blocked. In addition, the phonemes /e/ and /o/ had off-glides ([j] and [w], respectively) in free syllable. /ɛ/ and /ɔ/ had on-glides ([j] and [w]) in both free and blocked syllable. This system of allophones is illustrated in Schema I of Appendix C.

Although the criteria for the reconstruction of these phonemes and allophones are taken primarily from Mod. Vegl., research by Romance scholars gives further weight to the reconstruction. The Vegl. Lat. vowel system as presented is identical to that of the so-called Proto-West-Romance system.³ That is, Vegl. developed from a vowel system congruent to those offered as earlier stages of all West Romance languages. Veglia is only about 40 miles from Trieste, a trade center of the early centuries of the Christian era. The primary Roman road from Northern Italy to Dalmatia and Albania ran along the coast near Veglia. It is considered as further support for the analysis that the system reconstructed from different data is the same for Veglia as for nearby Northern Italy.⁴

W. von Wartburg argues that by the end of the fifth century the long variants of vowels in free syllable postulated for Vegl. were widespread in Latin.⁵ The trait of free syllable allophones [ej] and [ow] of /e/ and /o/ is also found in large areas of Northern Italy. It is normally a result of vowel differentiation, attributed by Wartburg to a Germanic superstratum. The probability of diffusion to nearby Veglia is high, further supporting the reconstruction of these allophones in the Latin of Veglia. Finally, the diphthongal realization [jɛ] and [wɔ] for /ɛ/ and /ɔ/ is frequently found in

---

³ I use the term Proto-West-Romance essentially as an equivalent of the traditional terms "Common Romance" and "Vulgar Latin". I refrain from entering the discussion of the value of the terms or of the significance of the system indicated, since such discussion is tangential to the problem at hand.

⁴ A more detailed discussion of this vowel system, in particular comparing it to the results offered by BARTOLI, is given in Appendix D, 79-84 and 86-87.

⁵ WARTBURG, 1950, 143-147.

Northern Italy, and especially in RRom., in both free and blocked positions.

B. *Consonants*.

Discussion of the history of the Vegl. consonant system is brief relative to that of the vowel system for the simple reason that Vegl. was quite conservative in its preservation of Latin consonants. Deserving of special attention are the loss of phonemic consonant length (see below, 43) and the palatalization of velar stops before front vowels (see below, 52-54).

The consonant system of the Latin spoken in Veglia prior to the beginning of PSCr. influence had the phonemes / p t k b d g f s r l n m/. It is also probable that, by this period, the system contained the palatalized phonemes /l' n' c z/ which had developed out of fusion of /l n k g/ with following /j/. (/k/ and /g/ maintained their stop articulation before the front vowels /i/, /e/, and /ɛ/ during this period.) These phonemes are postulated for the Latin of Veglia of Period One because the palatalization is common to all Romance languages, and is generally considered to have taken place throughout Latin prior to the seventh century, hence prior to the isolation of Vegl. from continental Latin. [6]

The consonant system featured phonemic consonant length.

---

[6] The fact that a given phonological development is general in Latin does not require that this change have taken place simultaneously in many areas, nor that it developed in one area and spread. A change may also occur in many separated points at different periods of time and subsequent spread from these points may obliterate all evidence of the separate development. Furthermore, changes which appear to be the same may take place in different areas, but have completely unrelated structural causes.

Therefore, it is possible (though not probable, I believe), that the palatalized phonemes arising from fusion of consonant and /j/ developed after the seventh century in Vegliote. The dating of this phonological development has no effect on the remainder of the analysis.

CHAPTER SEVEN

PERIOD TWO:
THE EARLIEST SERBO-CROATIAN INFLUENCE

Serbo-Croatian, spoken in Dalmatian from the seventh century until today, has had important effects on the history of Vegl. It was therefore necessary to study in detail the history of SCr. and to attempt to describe its possible bilingual effect on Vegl.

The reconstructions, the results of which are presented in this and the succeeding two chapters, were made on the basis of evidence from Mod. SCr., and of comparative evidence from other Slavic languages.[1]

A. *The early Serbo-Croatian phonemic system.*

The vowel system of PSCr. as it was spoken by the Slavic immigrants flowing into Dalmatia in the seventh century and thereafter was an eight vowel system. It had the contrasts of high:low, front:back, and long:short. Labialization was a marginal feature in this system (see Appendix C, II).

The phoneme /æ:/ was manifested phonetically by [jæ:].

The only feature of the consonant system of special interest here is the lack of phonemic consonant length, in which PSCr. contrasted with Vegl. Lat.

---

[1] My primary source works were: MEILLET, 1934; MARTINET, 1955, 349-375; LESKIEN, 1914; LUNT, 1959; and POPOVIĆ, 1960. The reconstruction as presented is essentially that of MAREŠ, 1956. I am particularly indebted to Prof. LADISLAV MATEJKA of the Department of Slavic Languages of the University of Michigan for assistance in the study of SCr.

B. *The effect on the Latin of Veglia.*

The possible effect of one language on another must be examined in terms of bilingual contact and the resultant possibility of transfer of structural features from one to the other. (Cf. the discussion of contrastive analysis, above, 24-26.)

1. The Vegliote merger of /a/ and /ɔ/.

A comparison of the vowel systems of Vegl. Lat. and PSCr. during the early period of contact (see Appendix A, I and II) reveals that native speakers of PSCr. had but two phonemes, /ɔ/ and /ɔ:/, with which to interpret the three Vegl. Lat. phonemes /a/, /ɔ/, and /o/. As a result, when attempting to speak Latin, native speakers of PSCr. would have difficulty making the distinction between the three Vegl. Lat. phonemes (cf. "under-differentiation", above, 25). After generations of bilingual contact, the result was the transfer of this lack of distinction to Vegl. Lat., and the merger of /a/ and /ɔ/.[2]

2. The loss of phonemic consonant length.

Since PSCr. lacked phonemic consonant length, native speakers of PSCr. would find it difficult to distinguish Vegl. Lat. long consonants from the corresponding short consonants. By a structural transfer identical to the one just described, Vegl. Lat. suffered a loss of phonemic consonant length, long consonants merging with the corresponding short ones.

3. Vowel differentiation.

An immediate result of the loss of phonemic consonant length was vowel differentiation. Since Vegl. Lat. long consonants blocked a preceding syllable and conditioned a short vowel allophone (short consonants conditioning a long allophone), when long consonants merged with short, the previous long and short vowel allophones occurred in contrastive opposition and therefore attained the status of separate phonemes.[3] The result of this Vegl. Lat.

---

[2] The basic PSCr. contrast of back:front led to the interpretation of Vegl. /a/ as a back vowel by speakers of PSCr. and aided its merger with /ɔ/.

[3] This process would be identified by HOENIGSWALD (1960, 93-95) as a "secondary phonemic split"; i.e., a phonemic split resulting from the merger of conditioning environments.

development was a system of phonemic vowel length, with long vowels occurring in previously free syllable, short vowels in blocked (see App. C, III).[4] This description is identical with that of Haudricourt and Juilland for preliterary French.[5] Their hypothetical illustration of the process is the following: */atta/ : /ata/>*/ata/ : /a : ta/.[6]

One important feature of this new system of phonemic vowel length is that previous allophones with respect to on- and off-glides continue in the corresponding positions in the new system: /e:/ and /o:/ are manifested by [e:j] and [o:w]; /ɛ:/ and /ɛ/ by [jɛ:] and [jɛ]; /ɔ:/ and /ɔ/ by [wɔ:] and [wɔ] (see App. C, III).

The development of phonemic vowel length in Vegl. Lat. has been described here has a purely internal result of the loss of phonemic consonant length (i.e., loss of Vegl. Lat. consonant length phonemicized Vegl. Lat. vowel length). Note, however, that external influence must have played an equally large role in the development of vowel length, since the result is congruence between the Vegl. and PSCr. systems: both now have phonemic vowel length, but lack phonemic consonant length.

Weinreich's term "underdifferentiation" would apply to the inability of PSCr. speakers to distinguish long from short consonants, but the changes may also be viewed as a result of "reinterpretation of distinctions" (above, 25). Speakers of PSCr. could

---

[4] Blocked syllables did not disappear from the language, since a cluster of two different consonants continued to block a preceding syllable. However, occurrence in contrastive environment in one position is sufficient to establish the long : short phonemic contrast, and long and short allophones in all other positions are reinterpreted phonemically.

[5] HAUDRICOURT—JUILLAND, 1949, 36.

[6] Although the process of development of phonemic vowel length is the same, the development in Vegl. must be considered different from any Western Romance change because of one important aspect: since there is no occurrence in Vegl. of the sonorization of intervocalic voiceless stops nor of the spirantization of intervocalic voiced stops (developments which are generally considered to be related to the loss of phonemic consonant length in Vegl. must be considered a non-Western development. Therefore, although the *process* by which the phonemic vowel length developed may be identical with certain West Romance developments, the original phonological stimulus (i.e., loss of phonemic consonant length) is quite unrelated. See also below, 87.

distinguish between Vegl. Lat. */atta/ and */ata/, but they would hear them as if they were phonemically /ata/ and /a:ta/. Because this would also be the form taken by the *production* of such a minimal pair by a native speaker of PSCr., it was possible for the phonemic feature of vowel length to be transferred to Vegl. Lat.

CHAPTER EIGHT

PERIOD THREE:
LATER SERBO-CROATIAN CHANGES AND THEIR
REFLECTION IN VEGLIOTE

A. *Changes in Serbo-Croatian in Period Three.*

1. In this period, the simplification of a diphthong (/ow/) brings a new phoneme /u/ into the SCr. system.
2. Labialization becomes a distinctive feature in the system.
3. Former /ï:/ is fronted to /ɨ/.
4. Former /ï/ and /i/, the so-called "jers", are lost in certain positions, and merge in /ə/ in other positions.
5. Phonemic length is lost from the system, vowel quality replacing previous phonemic quantity.

A representation of the results of these changes is given in Appendix C, IV.[1]

---

[1] At this point it is possible to offer some estimates of chronology for Periods Two and Three. Because of textual attestation, Slavicists generally believe that the simplification of the diphthong /ow/ to /u/ was complete by the ninth century. The merger of the jers was most probably complete by the eleventh century. The fronting of /i:/ > /ɨ/ is placed prior to the eleventh century. Because of the possible separation in time of these developments, Schema IV must be considered to represent the phonemic system at the end of this period.

Thus, Period Three can be considered to embrace the time from the ninth to the eleventh centuries, Period Two from the sixth to the ninth. It should be evident, however, that these are rough estimates. The reason for establishing periods of development is primarily procedural. The periods give some order to the presentation.

B. *The effects on Vegliote.*

1. The fronting of Vegl. Lat. /u/.

Mod. Vegl. shows that, at one point in its history Vegl. Lat. /u/ had a palatal articulation. The evidence for this articulation is that the Mod. Vegl. equivalent of Lat. /u/ is /oj/ which shows the palatal excreted consonant /j/ rather than /w/, and that Vegl. Lat. /k/ has the same palatal result /č/ in Mod. Vegl. before both former /u/ and /i/: e.g. Vegl. Lat /kalkina/, /oskuro/ > Mod. Vegl. /kalčajna/, /sčojr/.

Since Vegl. Lat /u/ and PSCr. /ï:/ must have been equated in bilingual speech from the earliest contact onward (each represents the high-back phoneme of its respective system), the fronting of Vegl. Lat. /u/ > /ü/ must be associated with the fronting of PSCr. /ï/ > /i/ in Period Three.

2. The loss of phonemic vowel length.

During Period Three, Vegl., parallel to SCr., loses phonemic vowel length. Although it is possible that the Vegl. and the SCr. loss of length occurred at different times and that the loss in the two languages is unrelated, the probability is great of a causal relation between the two developments, since relative chronology places the two in the same general period, and since the continued intimate bilingual contact is obvious.

3. The phonemicization of [j] and [w].

The twelve possible phonemes resulting from loss of phonemic vowel length were soon reduced to five by a series of phonemic mergers.

Let us turn our attention to the merger of former /e:/ and /e/. The phoneme /e:/ was manifested phonetically by [e:j], /e/ by [e]. That is to say, the allophonic off-glide on /e:/ was conditioned by phonemic length. When phonemic length was lost and /e:/ merged with /e/, pairs of words previously distinguished minimally by vowel length were now distinguished by the off-glide. The off-glide occurs in contrastive environments and attains the phonemic status of consonantal /j/.

The development /e:/ > /ej/ offers a pattern for the reinterpretation of all long vowels: long vowel becomes vowel plus semiconsonant. In this same pattern /o:/ (= [o:w]) > /ow/; /i:/ > /ij/; and /ü:/ > /üj/. In the case of /ɛ:/ (=[jɛ:]) and /ɔ:/ (=[wɔ:]), this phonemic reinterpretation by Vegl. speakers of long vowels leads to a shift of vocality:[2] [jɛ:] > [iɛ̣], [wɔ:] > [uɔ̣]. (See App. C, Va.) That the stress shift is the result of the extension of a pattern can be amplified as follows: With the former long vowels now represented by /ij/, /ej/, /üj/, and /ow/ (i.e., with the shape VC), the CV forms [jɛ] and [wɔ] constitute anomalies in the system. With the shift of vocality, these forms are interpreted as VC, and thus [iɛ̣] and [uɔ̣] conform to the pattern. (The ultimate simplification of these two forms to /i/ and /u/ indicate that at some point [ɛ] and [ɔ] were interpreted as /j/ and /w/; hence /jɛ/ > /iɛ̣/ > /ij/ > /i/ and /wɔ/ > /uɔ̣/ > /uw/ > /u/.[3]

Languages often change by means of the extension of a pattern established in one portion of the system, and according to my description the Vegl. changes /jɛ:/ > /iɛ̣/ and /wɔ:/ > /uɔ̣/ are a result of such an extension. However, I do not imply that such extensions are in any way predictable, or that any given pattern *must* spread throughout a system. I have attempted to explain what happened in Vegl., and how it happened, but I demur at attempting the why.

4. Phonemic mergers.

During the period in which the loss of phonemic vowel length took place, in addition to the phonemicization of /j/ and /w/, there occurred a series of phonemic mergers. The syllabic elements of /ij/, /ej/, /e/ and /jɛ/ merge in /e/; the syllabic elements of /wɔ/ and /ow/ merge in /ɔ/; and those of /ü/ and /üj/ in /ü/. The results of these mergers are summarized in Appendix C, Schema Vb. This schema is presented only as an illustration and as a summary of what has just been discussed. No implication is intended that the system represented did in fact exist. There is no way of knowing if the changes described occurred at the same time, and no way of ascribing a synchronic reality to the schema.

---

[2] The term "shift of vocality" is used to refer to the reinterpretation as a vowel by speakers of Vegl. of the first element of /jɛ/ and /wɔ/. Since the second element becomes a semi-vowel, a shift of stress is necessarily a feature of this change.

[3] The development of /je/ > /i/ in the Romagnolo dialects of Italy is considered by Schürr (1952, 89) to be a result of vowel differentiation. The development of /jɛ/ > /i/ and /wɔ/ > /u/ in Vegl. also arises from vowel differentiation, although my inclusion of more detailed explication makes the relation appear somewhat indirect.

CHAPTER NINE

PERIOD FOUR:
THE CHANGES WHICH PRODUCED MODERN VEGLIOTE

The system just described (Vb) suffers some remarkable phonemic shifts and mergers, the product of which is the Mod. Vegl. vowel system.

Periods Three and Four overlap slightly because certain of the changes have effects in both periods; it could be argued that the two periods are in fact one. However, because of the complexity of the changes, it is advisable that they be presented in two separate stages.

A. *Serbo-Croatian changes in Period Four.*

1. During this period, SCr. /æ/ (=[jæ]) disappears from the system through a merger with /i/. This development is restricted to the so-called I-dialects of SCr., but these dialects are spoken on the island of Veglia, and all along the adjacent mainland.[1] The significance for Vegl. is discussed below, 52.

2. SCr. /ɨ/ disappears from the system, also through a merger with /i/.

3. Finally, SCr. /ɔ/ and /ə/ merge in /a/.[2] (See Appendix C, Schemas IV and VI.)

---

[1] POPOVIĆ, 1960, 348.
[2] The SCr. changes /ɔ/ and /ə/ > /a/ take place most probably in the fourteenth century. All of the changes have taken place by the time of the SCr. texts of the fifteenth century. This gives a *terminus ante quem* for the

B. *Venetian.*

From the earliest days of the Ven. colonization of Dalmatia (i.e., in the eleventh century) until the present, the Ven. language had a seven vowel phonemic system: /i e ε a ɔ o u/.[3] The system lacked phonemic vowel length.

Most important for my discussion, Ven. had a phoneme /a/ in the low *central* position, contrasting in this respect with both Vegl. and SCr. of Period Three, and Ven. lacked any palatal or front correlate of Vegl. /ü/.

C. *Vegliote developments in Period Four.*

1. Internal description.

The shifts and mergers that take place in this period bring about the final Mod. Vegl. vowel system (see Appendix C, Vb and VIII).

a) Old Vegl.[4] /iε̯/ simplifies to Mod. Vegl. /i/, but does not merge with Old Vegl. /i/.

b) Old Vegl. /u̯o/ simplifies to Mod. Vegl. /u/ and merges with Old Vegl. /o/, which also shifts to /u/.[5]

c) Old Vegl. /e/ lowers to Mod. Vegl. /a/.

d) Old Vegl. /ɔ/ lowers to Mod. Vegl. /a/, where it merges with Old Vegl. /e/.

SCr. of Period Four, but the corresponding Vegl. changes may have taken place considerably later. Since Ven. influence is a feature of Period Four, and since this influence operated from the eleventh century to the present, Period Four may be considered to cover the time from the eleventh century on (cf. above, 46, n. 1).

[3] In many areas of Mod. Ven. these seven vowels have been reduced to five through a merger of /e/ and /ε/ on the one hand, and of /o/ and /ɔ/ on the other: Vidos, 1959, 141.

[4] The term "Old Vegl." is used henceforth to refer to the system of Vegl. in Period Three, represented in Schema V.

[5] There is no possibility of discerning why the Old Vegl. /u̯o/ and /o/ merge, but /iε̯/ and /i/ do not. Given a large enough corpus for the period of the change, analysis could theoretically show that the frequency of occurrence of the phonemes and the functional load of the opposition determined their merger or conservation. Without such data, a postulation in this direction is sheer guesswork. I am consequently limited to the description of which mergers took place and which did not.

e) Old Vegl. /ü/ shifts to Mod. Vegl. /o/.

The following schema is essentially a rearrangement in relative buccal position of Vb, with the arrows illustrating the changes just mentioned. [6]

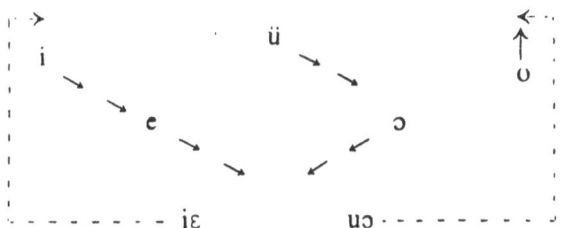

Given the simplification of Old Vegl. /iɛ̯/ > /i/ and its non-merger with Old Vegl. /i/, it is apparent that the phonetic similarity of the two i-type phonemes led to a confusion in the stream of speech, so that to conserve the opposition (or to keep minimal pairs distinct), Old Vegl. /i/ moved away from the [i] position toward /e/, which in its turn was able to move downward into the position vacated by /ɛ:/ upon its change to /iɛ̯/ > /i/.

By a similar process, as Old Vegl. /u̯ɔ/ simplified to /u/, /ɔ/ shifted downward toward /a/. In its turn, the /ɔ/ > /a/ shift, along with the shift /o/ > /u/ gave way before the movement of Old Vegl. /ü/ > /o/. [7]

2. External influences.

a) Serbo-Croatian.

Further insight into these Vegliote changes is gained by observing the close relation between them and SCr. shifts of the same period.

---

[6] The broken arrows are not used to indicate a phonemic shift but rather the simplification of /iɛ̯/ and /u̯ɔ/ to /i/ and /u/. It is now possible to point out that the apparent paradox of C.L. /ĕ/ = Mod. Vegl. /i/ and C.L. /ī/ = Mod. Vegl. /e/ was brought about by the shift of vocality already discussed (above, 48).

[7] These mutual adjustments offer some classical examples of "chain reaction". Cf. MARTINET, 1955, 59-62. Whether or not these chain reactions are "push-chains" or "drag-chains" is, of course, moot, since we can establish no logical or chronological priority for any of the shifts.

1) The Vegl. development /ε:/ > /iε/ > /i/ is paralleled by the SCr. change /æ:/ (=[jæ:]) > /i/ (above, 49). It would be very difficult to deny a causal relation between the two changes.

2) It has been shown that the early bilingual identification of Vegl. Lat. /u/ and PSCr. /ï:/ in Period Two caused Vegl. Lat. /u/ to front to /ü/ when PSCr. /ï:/ fronted to /i/. Consequently, when this SCr. correlate of Vegl. /ü/ is removed from the system, bilingual support for this phoneme disappears, permitting the shift of /ü/ > /o/.

3) When SCr. /ǝ/ and /ɔ/ merge, the original PSCr. contrast of back: front in the low area of the system is destroyed. This back: front contrast was considered an important factor in the backward shift of Vegl. Lat. /a/ and its merger with /ɔ/. Conversely, the loss of this contrast and the shift of /ɔ/ > /a/ in SCr. causes (or aids) a shift of /ɔ/ > /a/ in Vegl. The loss of the back: front contrast also aids the merger of Old Vegl. /e/ with /ɔ/ in Mod. Veg. /a/.

b) Venetian.

The increasing influence of Venetian is observable in these Vegl. shifts. (It is quite possible that Venetian was the prime mover for changes in both the Old Vegl. and the SCr. systems in Period Four.)

1) Since Venetian had no phoneme with which to associate Old Vegl. /ü/, speakers of Venetian interpreted the labial element of this vowel as its most important feature. The external influence of Venetian on Old Vegl. resulted in the shift of /ü/ into the back series.

2) The presence of /a/ in the Venetian system aided (and possibly caused) the shift and merger of Old Vegl. /e/ and /ɔ/ in Mod. Vegl. /a/. This would be a further example of bilingual underdifferentiation (see above, 25 and 43).

D. *Consonantal changes in Period Four.*

The final consonantal change from Old Vegl. to Mod. Vegl. is the development of the palatal phonemes /č/ and /ǧ/ for Vegl. Lat. /k/ and /g/ before /i/ and /ε/ (not /e/). The following schema presents the Mod. Vegl. results for /k/ and /g/ before front vowels:

Vegl. Lat.	kwi [8] ki	kwe ke	kwɛ kɛ
Type of syllable	blocked free	free blocked	blocked free
Mod. Vegl.	če čaj	kaj ka	ča či
Vegl. Lat.	gwi gi	gwe ge	gwɛ gɛ
Mod. Vegl.	ǧe ǧaj	gaj *ga	ǧa *ǧi

Martinet has explained the phonemicization of /č/ and /ǧ/ in Italian as an illustration of chain reaction.[9] For reasons unnecessary to argue here, Latin forms containing /kuj/ shifted vocality (> /kwi/). The result was an impending confusion with previous /kwi/, which adjusted to the difficulty by simplification to /ki/. This simplification forced a previous /ki/ to become palatalized to avoid further confusion. Thus, the three-way contrast was maintained: /kuj/ : /kwi/ : /ki/ > /kwi/ : /ki/ : /či/.

This structural explanation is not possible for Vegl., since Latin /kwi/ and /ki/, etc., had merged before the phonemicization took place. One must look for specifically Vegl. characteristics for the structural explanation of the development of /č/ and /ǧ/.

It is apparent from the schema presented above that /č/ and /ǧ/ developed before the merger of Old Vegl. /ij/ and /ej/, because the palatal phonemes occur before the former, but /k/ and /g/ remain before the latter. It is further suggested that at the time of the phonemicization of /č/ and /ǧ/, Old Vegl. /e/ had shifted far enough toward its Mod. Vegl. position /a/ so that a preceding /k/ or /g/ had a clearly non-palatal allophone. The phonological conditions under which /č/ and /ǧ/ attain phonemic status are (1) the merger of Old Vegl. /e/ and /jɛ/ (in Old Vegl. /e/, which shifts to Mod. Vegl. /a/), and (2) the absorption of /j/ in the preceding allophone of /k/ and /g/ (e.g., Old Vegl. /kjɛnto/ > Mod Vegl. /čant/, like Mod. Ital. /čelo/).[10]

---

[8] Latin /kw/ and /gw/ before front vowels have the same results in Mod. Vegl. as /k/ and /g/ before front vowels.

[9] MARTINET, 1955, 60-61.

[10] (1946, 1-3) Bonfante argued that the lack of palatalization of *Lat.* /k/ and /g/ before *Lat.* /e/ in Vegl. was due to the geographic position of Veglia

When the vowel merger takes place and /j/ is absorbed in [k'] and [g'], these palatal allophones of /k/ and /g/ before /je/ occur in contrast to the non-palatal allophones before the downward-shifting /e/. Occurrence in this contrastive environment establishes the palatal allophones as the phonemes which result in Mod. Vegl. /č/ and /ǧ/: e.g. /ke:/ : /kje/ > /kæ/ : /k'æ/ > /ka/ : /ča/. With the establishment of /k'/ and /g'/ as separate phonemes, the palatal allophones of former /k/ and /g/ before Old Vegl. /i/ and /ü/ are reinterpreted as these new phonemes: Old Vegl. /ki/ > /k'i/ > Mod. Vegl. /če/, etc.

---

on the periphery of the phonological wave of palatalization, and consequently in an area where the wave was weak. In my analysis, the palatalization of Vegl. /k/ takes places before *Vegl.* /i/ and /e/, but not before Vegl. /a/, a condition identical to that of other Romance languages. From the structural point of view, then, Bonfante's argument is inaccurate.

PART THREE

APPENDICES

Appendix A

PHONEMIC ANALYSIS OF MODERN VEGLIOTE

I. THE DATA.

Bartoli included in *Das Dalmatische* not only his own transcription of the language of the last Vegliote speaker, but also transcriptions done by all previous researchers. In his zeal to include everything in his book, he duly published all data from whatever source, including the three words that one informant remembered having heard years previously.

Bartoli was fortunate in being able to spend considerable time with Antonio Udina, the last speaker of Vegliote, and he managed to transcribe a corpus of about 10,000 words of running conversation. This corpus represents the work of one linguist with one informant. Therefore it contains the most reliable data available and the present analysis is based on it.

The text comprises about eighteen half-pages in folio, the second half of each page being taken up by the Italian translation. Bartoli used a phonetic alphabet unfamiliar in present-day American linguistics (e.g. Bartoli's z = [ẓ], ṡ = [z], etc.); but he includes a phonetic chart (II, 264) which gives the phonetic equivalents in terms of Italian words. In the present work, Bartoli's alphabet has been changed in accordance with the phonetic chart on page 9, above.

The phonemic analysis of a written text imposes a number of restrictions on the analysis which are not present when the linguist works directly with an informant. For example, Bartoli's corpus shows no intonation markings. Only a vague idea can be gained from his use of interrogative and exclamation marks, commas, and periods. Only an approximation of juncture can be made from spaces, commas, and periods. He occasionally uses a hyphen, which appears to indicate internal open juncture, but whose inconsistent usage permits no conclusion. The result is that the phonemic analysis can deal only with segmental (consonant and vowel) phonemes.

Further difficulties are imposed by the informant himself. The most important factor is that Udina had not spoken Vegl. for some twenty years, and he tended, especially early in the period of contact with Bartoli, to use Venetian words directly, or to "Vegliotize" Venetian words. The result, of course, is considerable variation. Aside from speaking Venetian, a language very similar to Vegl., in his everyday life, Udina knew a little Church Latin, having served as a minor ecclesiastical official; he knew Friulian because he had worked in a Friulian speaking area of Italy; and he spoke Serbo-Croatian well.

In addition to being hard to handle as an informant, according to Bartoli's description, he was a little deaf, and he had no teeth. The lack of teeth must have lead to a certain amount of misunderstanding, especially of the sibilant sounds.

Despite these shortcomings of the data, the corpus is large enough to permit a structural analysis which reveals the phonemic system of Vegl. with a fair degree of reliability.

II. THE ANALYSIS.

A. *Consonants.*

1. The Mod. Vegl. reflected in the phonetic corpus has twenty two consonant phonemes:

p	t	k
b	d	g
f	s	
v	z	
	ç	č
	ʒ̧	ǧ
m	n	n'
	l	l'
	r	
w		j

2. Examples of contrasting environments.

Minimal pairs were not found for every contrasting pair of phonemes. Where no minimal pair was found, a number of pairs were used as evidence of contrast in analogous environments.[1]

A	B	C	D
/p:b/	ku̯arp	/kwarp/	'corpo'
	ku̯arb	/kwarb/	'corvo'
	bu͡o̯r	/bur/	'boreo'
	pu͡o̯r	/pur/	'pare'
/k:g/	ku̯al	/kwal/	'collo'
	gu̯al	/gwal/	'gola'

---

[1] A = contrasting phonemes; B = Bartoli's transcription; C = my analysis; and D = Bartoli's Italian translation.

A	B	C	D
	gu̯arn	/gwarn/	'frassino'
	ku̯arn	/kwarn/	'corno'
/t : d/	tu̯ọta	/tuta/	'padre'
	du̯ọte	/dute/	'date'
	drante	/drante/	'dentro'
	trante	/trante/	'trenta'
/f : v/	feŋ	/fen/	'fino'
	veŋ	/ven/	'vino'
	fi̯ar	/fjar/	'ferro'
	vi̯ar	/vjar/	'vero' ²
/b : v/	buŋ	/bun/	'buono'
	vuŋ	/vun/	'avena'
	ču̯arv	/čwarv/	'guercio'
	ku̯arb	/kwarb/	'corvo'
/l : l'/	fu̯al'	/fwal'/	'foglia'
	ku̯al	/kwal/	'collo'
	nol'a	/nol'a/	'nulla'
	kola	/kola/	'quella'
/l' : j/³	vu̯al'	/vwal'/	'olio'
	vu̯ai̯	/vwaj/	'oggi'

---

² The curious reader may find that a number of the examples used in this analysis do not represent the normal development as indicated by large groups of words. Thus the normal Vegl. reflex for C.L. *verum* would be /vajr/. These variations from the norm are to be considered a result of the informant's imperfect recollection of Vegl., and his tendency to "Vegliotize" Ven. words. However, these words represent the phonological possibilities of Mod. Vegl. and offer legitimate evidence for establishing phonemic contrasts.

³ A frequent variation between the Vegl. phonemes /l'/, /j/, and /ǧ/ in the data is attributable to the influence of Ven. in the speech of the informant. Ven. lacks /l'/, and words having this phoneme in standard Ital. (and Vegl.) show either /j/ or /ǧ/, and sometimes both: E.g., Rosamani cites the reflex of Lat. *olio* as *ojo* in some dialects, *oǧo* in others. Both forms may be heard in Trieste.

PHONEMIC ANALYSIS OF MODERN VEGLIOTE 61

A	B	C	D
	pul'a	/pul'a/	'paglia'
	pula	/pula/	'penis'
/č:ɛ/	ɛu̯ǫnka	/ɛunka/	'manca'
	čenk	/čenk/	'cinque'
	spi̯aɛ	/spjaɛ/	'specie'
	bu̯ač	/bwač/	'bocca'
/ǧ:ẓ/	ǧara	/ǧara/	'era'
	ẓar	/ẓar/	'andare'
	ǧinakli	/ǧinakli/	'ginocchi'
	ẓigu̯ǫnt	/ẓigunt/	'gigante'
/ẓ:z/	su̯anẓ	/swanẓ/	'sugna'
	su̯arz	/swarz/	'sorcio'
	ẓu̯ante	/ẓwante/	'giunte'
	zu̯ark	/zwark/	'sicciolo'
/ɛ:ẓ/	ɛar	/ɛar/	'sera'
	ẓar	/ẓar/	'andare'
	ɛu̯ǫŋka	/ɛunka/	'manca'
	ẓu̯ǫra	/ẓura/	'orcio'
/s:z/	su̯ark	/swark/	'sorgo'
	zu̯ark	/zwark/	'sicciolo'
	kosai̯k	/kosajk/	'come'
	koi̯za	/kojza/	'così'
/č:ǧ/	lačar	/lačar/	'sgombero'
	leǧar	/leǧar/	'leggiero'
	čonk	/čonk/	'cinque'
	ǧu̯ǫŋ	/ǧun/	'Giovanne'
/r:l/	rau̯da	/rawda/	'ruota'
	lau̯da	/lawda/	'loda'
	lu̯at	/lwat/	'latte'
	ru̯at	/rwat/	'rotto'

A	B	C	D
/m:n/	nu̯at	/nwat/	'notte'
	mu̯at	/mwat/	'muto'
	ni̯at	/njat/	'netto'
	mi̯at	/mjat/	'metto'
/n:n'/	pai̯na	/pajna/	'pena'
	vai̯n'a	/vajn'a/	'vigna'
	panu̯ada	/panwada/	'panata'
	pan'u̯oka	/pan'uka/	'pagnotta'

3. Problems of interpretation.

a) Syllabic [r̥] is an allophone of the phoneme /r/. It occurs only in penultimate or final position and is always preceded by a consonant.

    [telegr̥f] 'telegrafo'
    [ćianr̥]   'cenere'
    [majestr̥] 'maestro'

The occurrence of this sound is not a reflection of normal Vegl. phonology, and is probably a result of interference of the informant's knowledge of SCr.

b) [ŋ] is an allophone of /n/, since it occurs only word-finally, or before a velar consonant:

  [puŋ]   /pun/   'pane'
  [buŋ]   /bun/   'buono'
  [oŋgla] /ongla/ 'unghia'

c) The phonemes /j/ and /w/ deserve special attention. /w/ is represented in the data only by the graph u̯. Alternate interpretations of the data would be that the sound represented by the graph u̯ is an allophone of /u/, or that it is a separate semi-vocalic phoneme /u̯/. The *sound* [w] (my transcription of Bartoli's graph u̯) is not a submember of /u/, since /u/ would then operate as both a consonant and a vowel. Structural patterning shows that [w] occurs in normally consonantal positions, e.g:

CCVC			CVCC		
stal	/stal/	'stella'	pask	/pask/	'pesce'
swal	/swal/	'suola'	pawk	/pawk/	'poco'

Perhaps most important, structural patterning shows that Vegl. does not permit word-initial stressed vowels,[4] and [w] often occurs initially. Further, [w] shows some free variation with /v/ in this position: e.g. /wapto/ ∼ /vapto/ = 'otto'; /waklo/ ∼ /vaklo/ = 'occhio', etc.

Because it is always non-syllabic, and because it always occurs in a consonantal slot, [w] is interpreted as a manifestation of the semi-consonant phoneme /w/. It would be acceptable to include both /w/ and /u̯/ in the phonemic inventory, but this merely increases the inventory without adding effectiveness to the analysis.

The phoneme /j/ is represented in Bartoli's data by the graphs j and i̯, and it has a distribution parallel to that of /w/:

e.g	CCVCC		
	pluŋka	/plunka/	'lastra di pietra'
	prai̯sa	/prajsa/	'presa'
	pi̯aska	/pjaska/	'peska'
	pi̯ai̯ta	/pjajta/	'piega'

Bartoli's [i̯] occurs only in consonantal slots and it is in complementary distribution with [j], since he uses [j] only between syllabic vowels or in initial position (e.g. [sajai̯ta] = 'saeta'; [ju̯ǫpa] = 'ape'), and he never uses [i̯] in these positions (e.g. [vai̯ta] = 'vita'; [bi̯al] = 'bello').

For these reasons [i̯] and [j] are analyzed as manifestations of the semi-consonant phoneme /j/. The alternative of separating /j/ and /i̯/ adds no effectiveness to the analysis.

---

[4] Words which have initial stressed vowels in other Romance languages normally have /j/ + vowel in Vegl.: /jal/ = 'egli', /jwalt/ = 'alto', /juv/ = 'uovo', /jojn/ = 'uno', etc. Occasionally /v/ is found instead of /j/ in words which have initial back vowels in other Romance languages: /vaklo/ = 'occhio', /vapto/ = 'otto'.

B. *Vowels.*

1. The Mod. Vegl. reflected in Bartoli's phonetic transcriptions has a system of five vowel phonemes:

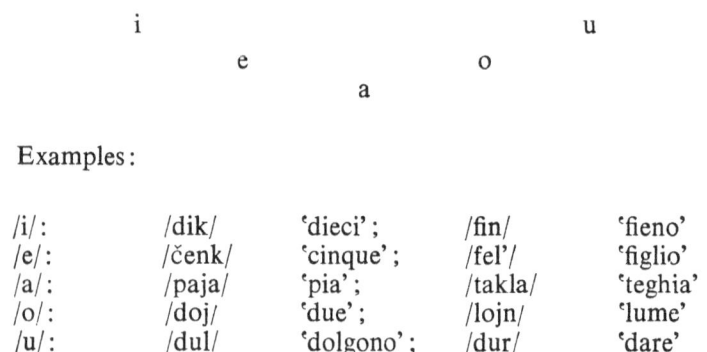

Examples:

/i/:	/dik/	'dieci';	/fin/	'fieno'
/e/:	/čenk/	'cinque';	/fel'/	'figlio'
/a/:	/paja/	'pia';	/takla/	'teghia'
/o/:	/doj/	'due';	/lojn/	'lume'
/u/:	/dul/	'dolgono';	/dur/	'dare'

2. Discussion.

a) Bartoli uses three graphs which could represent variants of /i/: i, i̯, and j. The sounds represented by i̯ and j have already been discussed with the rest of the consonants.

b) The phoneme /u/ is manifested in the transcriptions by [u] and [u̯o͡]. The fact that Bartoli's graph [u̯o͡] represents a sound which is a variant of /u/ is a crucial point in the reconstruction of Vegl. Lat. The primary evidence for this allophonic relation is that of the consistent frequent free variation between [u̯o͡] and [u].

[tuta] ~ [tu̯o͡ta]	'padre'
[animul] ~ [animu̯o͡l]	'animale'
etc.	

Bartoli describes the sound represented by his graph [u̯o͡] as being like a long, open [u], but clearly contrasting with the Ital. [wo] in 'buono', etc. He further relates an incident in which he pronounced a Vegl. word, using the Italian pronunciation of *uo*, at which point his informant corrected him, and spelled the word with *u*.

Because the data contain no examples of contrast between [u̯o͡] and [u], since they occur in free variation, and because the informant testifies to their "sameness", these phones must be two allophones of /u/.

c) Bartoli uses no symbols which could be interpreted to represent variants of the phonemes /e/, /a/, and /o/. Since these sounds occur in consistent contrast, their phonemic integrity is unquestionable.

C. *Distribution.*

1. Vowels.

All vowels occur in all syllabic positions in the word. However, vowels in stressed word-initial position are severely restricted in frequency and usually represent loan words.

2. Consonants.

a) Syllable structure.

The following list illustrates all Vegl. syllable types with respect to distribution of consonants:

CV	e.g. /pi/	'piede'
CCV	/ple/	'piu'
CCCV	/struta/	'strada'
CVC	/mun/	'mano'
CCVC	/plaɛ/	'piazza'
CCCVC	/spjak/	'specchio'
CCCCVC	/sklwav/	'servo'
CVCC	/pask/	'pesce'
CCVCC	/stunk/	'stanco'
CCCVCC	/stwart/	'storto'
CCCCVCC	/strwanɛ/	'stronzo'

b) Syllable-initial consonants and consonant clusters.

The following represents a total listing of consonants which occur at the beginning of the syllable:

1) CV: All consonants may occur singly at the beginning of a syllable.

2) CCV:

/bj/	e.g. /bjal/	'bello'
/bl/	/blare/	'volere'
/br/	/brud/	'brodo'
/bw/	/bwalp/	'volpe'

/dj/	/djante/	'dente'
/dr/	/drat/	'dritto'
/dw/	/dwag/	'doga'
/čw/	/čwarv/	'corvo'
/fj/	/fjat/	'fetta'
/fl/	/flunk/	'fianco'
/fr/	/frutro/	'fratello'
/fw/	/fwal'a/	'foglia'
/gl/	/glajba/	'gleba'
/gr/	/grun/	'grano'
/gw/	/gwab/	'gobbo'
/jw/	/jwalb/	'bianco'
/kj/	/kjur/	'chiaro'
/kl/	/kluv/	'chiave'
/kr/	/krojt/	'crudo'
/kw/	/kwant/	'conto'
/lw/	/lwat/	'latte'
/mj/	/mjarla/	'merlo'
/mw/	/mwart/	'morte'
/nj/	/njat/	'netto'
/nw/	/nwat/	'notte'
/pj/	/pjas/	'pezzo'
/pl/	/plajn/	'pieno'
/pr/	/prajma/	'prima'
/pw/	/pwast/	'posto'
/rj/	/rjast/	'resto'
/rw/	/rwat/	'roto'
/sč/	/sčunta/	'squama'
/sj/	/sjanpro/	'sempre'
/sk/	/skarpajna/	'scorpina'
/sf/	/sfiluɛ/	'sfilata'
/sl/	/slungut/	'allungato'
/sp/	/spajka/	'spica'
/st/	/stal/	'stella'
/sw/	/swalt/	'soldo'
/sv/	/svolúa/	'volavano'
/tj/	/tjasta/	'testa'
/tr/	/tra/	'tre'
/tw/	/twant/	'tanto'
/vj/	/vjant/	'vento'
/vw/	/vwalt/	'volte'
/ɛj/	/ɛjarč/	'cecchio'
/ʒw/	/ʒwant/	'giunte'
/ɛw/	/ɛwap/	'zoppo'

3) CCCV: /drj/ /drjaɛ/ 'treccia'
/frw/ /frwant/ 'fronte'
/grw/ /grwas/ 'grosso'
/krj/ /krjúa/ 'grida'
/plw/ /plwaja/ 'pioggia'
/prw/ /prwant/ 'pronto'
/prj/ /prjas/ 'presto'
/skw/ /skwal'/ 'scoglio'
/sfr/ /sfris/ 'frego'
/skj/ /skjat/ 'schietto'
/skl/ /sklop/ 'schioppo'
/skr/ /skrit/ 'scritto'
/spj/ /spjaɛ/ 'specie'
/spw/ /spwarta/ 'sporta'
/spl/ /splojma/ 'spuma'
/str/ /strat/ 'stretto'
/stw/ /stwal/ 'tavola'
/stj/ /stjas/ 'stesso'
/zvw/ /zvwad/ 'vuota'
/trw/ /trwank/ 'tronco'

4) CCCCV: /strw/ /strwanɛ/ 'stronzo'
/sklw/ /sklwav/ 'servo'

c) Syllable-final consonants and consonant clusters.

The following is a complete list of all consonants which occur at the end of the syllable: [5]

1) VC: All consonants occur in this position.

2) VCC: /jd/ /fajd/ 'fiede'
/jk/ /lojk/ 'luce'
/jl/ /majl/ 'miglio'
/jm/ /flojm/ 'fiume'
/jn/ /fajn/ 'fino'
/js/ /majs/ 'mese'
/jt/ /sajt/ 'sete'
/lb/ /jwalb/ 'bianco'
/lm/ /kwalm/ 'tetto'
/lp/ /bwalp/ 'volpe'
/ls/ /pwals/ 'polso'
/lt/ /jult/ 'alto'

---

[5] Since no indication is given in the data for medial syllable juncture, all the information in this section had to come from word final clusters.

/mn/	/samn/	'sonno'
/mp/	/limp/	'lampi'
/nb/	/gunb/	'gambe'
/nč/	/vjanč/	'vinci'
/nɛ/	/uzwanɛ/	'uso'
/nd/	/grund/	'grande'
/nf/	/zn'unf/	'nasino'
/nk/	/lank/	'legno'
/np/	/tjanp/	'tempo'
/nr/	/ɛjanr/	'cenere'
/ns/	/gruns/	'granchio'
/nt/	/djant/	'dente'
/rb/	/kwarb/	'corvo'
/rɛ/	/twarɛ/	'torcia'
/rd/	/vjard/	'verde'
/rf/	/fwarf/	'forbici'
/rk/	/bwark/	'barca'
/rl/	/twarl/	'trottola'
/rm/	/vjarm/	'verme'
/rn/	/kwarn/	'corno'
/rp/	/kwarp/	'corpo'
/rs/	/diskwars/	'discorso'
/rt/	/čart/	'certo'
/rv/	/čwarv/	'guercio'
/rẓ/	/twarẓ/	'a zonzo'
/sk/	/pask/	'pesce'
/st/	/kwast/	'vitto'
/sp/	/nusp/	'naspo'
/tr/	/litr/	'litro'
/wd/	/bawd/	'voce'
/wk/	/krawk/	'croce'
/wl/	/djawl/	'diabolo'
/wn/	/sawn/	'suono'
/wr/	/sawr/	'sorella'
/ws/	/straws/	'strozza' (Ven.)

3) VCCC: There are only a few instances of syllable-final three-consonant clusters.[6] All of such clusters include the syllabic [r̥] considered to represent interference from SCr.

/grf/	/telegrf/	'telegrafo'
/str/	/mistr/	'maestro'

---

[6] Groups of three consonants occur medially but normally across what appears to be syllable junctures: /sanglo/ = [san·glo] = 'singolo'.

D. Frequency of occurrence.

The following figures represent the number of occurrences of each phoneme per thousand words of running text.

1. Vowels.

	STRESSED	UNSTRESSED	TOTAL
/a/	170	368	538
/u/	194	102	296
/e/	24	272	296
/i/	20	164	184
/o/	20	120	140

2. Consonants.

/r/	248	/b/	66
/l/	232	/f/	64
/k/	224	/d/	46
/j/	222	/č/	34
/t/	200	/ɛ/	28
/n/	196	/g/	22
/p/	136	/z/	22
/s/	102	/ʒ/	16
/w/	84	/l'/	10
/m/	74	/n'/	7
/v/	72	/ǧ/	4

E. Phonemic transcription.

The transcription is based on Bartoli, II, ss. 32, 33. The following symbols are arbitrarily assigned to Bartoli's punctuation to give a rough approximation of pauses:

/ = comma (phrase group?)
// = period, colon, semicolon (breath group?)
/// = paragraph (discourse juncture?)

///prájma de le mojér ju ve rakontúa jale prájma kawk avás il géler// kosájk/ kwátri kordjál inbotonúte jojna de jojna kal e jojna de la júltra// fero inbotonúte koste kwatri kordjál// fero rwás el géler// el géler// el géler fero kosájk/ apjárt/ ke tóč el pját se vedúa// el géler fero kojza jojna kapotín// kawk le avás jojn faẓolét tóč bjánk/ ma la fjásta/ sapájte/ le portúa kóst///

///per kotúl le portúa fénta kawk el nókol el pins/ na fenta tára/ la travjársa le portúa kójza ke le pwárta mut// mut le ju tornút portúr kojza ke fero nel tjánp vetrún// nawne nánka dík jájn ke le portúa la travjársa strjáta e mut le pwárta kojza ke portúa le vetrúne/ prájma///

Prima delle donne ve racconto. Una volta avevano qui il corpetto: così, quattro cordelle abbottonate una da una parte e una dall'altra. Erano abbottonate queste quattro cordelle. Era rosso il geler. Il geler era così, aperto, che tutto il petto si vedeva. Il geler era come una giacca. Qui avevano un fazzoletto tutto bianco; ma questo, badate, portavano alla festa.

Per (la) gonnella portavano fin qui alla nocella del piede, non fino a terra. Il grembiule portavano come portano adesso. Ora sono ritornate al tempo antico. Non son neppure dieci anni che portavano il grembiule stretto ed ora lo portano come portavano prima le vecchie.

APPENDIX B

LATIN-VEGLIOTE SOUND CORRESPONDENCES

As has already been indicated (above, 58, and 60, n. 2) the data present problems of interpretation due to the variety of forms found for many words. And illustration of how the informant "Vegliotized" Venetian words may be found in the comparison of the Mod. Vegl. and Mod. Ven. vowel correspondences with Latin. Using hypothetical examples, since no minimal quadruplets exist, compare:

LAT.	VEN.		VEGL.
/-ēna/	/-ena/		/-ajna/
/-ēnna/	/-ena/		/-anə/
/-ĕna/	/-ena/	(or /-ɛna/)	/-ina/
/-ĕnna/	/-ena/	(or /-ɛna/)	/-jana/
/-ōla/	/-ola/		/-awla/
/-ōlla/	/-ola/		/-ula/
/-ŏla/	/-ola/	(or /-ɔla/)	/-ula/
/-ŏlla/	/-ola/	(or /-ɔla/)	/-wala/

Thus if Bartoli's informant, in his imperfect memory of Vegl., were to produce a nonce-form based on Ven. /pena/ and /pola/, his utterance might take any of the four possible forms: */pajna/, */pana/, */pina/, or */pjana/, and */pawla/, */pula/, or */pwala/. In effect, we find in the data many examples of variants such as the following: Mod. Vegl. /tun/∼/tawn/∼/twan/ = "thunder" (Cf. Ven. /ton/).

The procedure for penetrating the obscuring element caused by such variations in the data to arrive at Latin-Vegliote sound correspondences relies on searching for items which occur several times in the data with no variation, and on an attention to consistency of pattern. Care must be exercised not to accept as proof single items which may be one of the nonce-forms produced by the informant. Haphazard choice of citations from the data without regard to patterning would permit proof of practically anything about Mod. Vegl.

The sound correspondences presented here are essentially those offered by Bartoli. The points at which my findings differ from his are discussed in Appendix D.

I. VOWELS.

A. *Stressed vowels.*

LAT. MOD. VEGL.   EXAMPLES

/ū/	fr	/oj/	durum	/dojr/	sputum	/spojt/
			flumen	/flojm/	crudum	/krojt/
			lucem	/lojk/	lunam	/lojna/
			udum	/jojt/	uvam	/jojva/
	bl	/o/	justum	/jost/	exsuctum	/sot/
/ŭ/	fr	/aw/	crucem	/krawk/	supra	/sawpra/
			ducem	/dawk/	gulam	/gawla/
			jugum	/zawk/		
	bl	/u/	cepullam	/kapul/	pulpam	/pulp/
			autumnus	/awtun/	buccam	/buka/
			nullum	/nul/	bullae	/bule/
			multum	/mult/	plumbum	/plunb/
/ō/	fr	/aw/	horam	/jawra/	vocem	/bawd/
			solem	/sawl/	soror	/sawr/
			-orem	/-awr/	-onem	/-awn/
	bl	/u/	formam	/furma/	soricem	/surko/
/ŏ/	fr	/u/	bonum	/bun/	focum	/fuk/
			locum	/luk/	ovum	/juv/
			dolet	/dul/	coquere	/kukro/
	bl	/wa/	postum	/pwast/	fortem	/fwart/
			longam	/lwanga/	corpus	/kwarp/
			mortem	/mwart/	collum	/kwal/

LATIN-VEGLIOTE SOUND CORRESPONDENCES EXAMPLES

/ă/	fr	/u/	dare	/dur/	panem	/pun/
			palum	/pul/	caput	/kup/
			apem	/jupa/	stratam	/strut/
	bl	/wa/	pastum	/pwast/	cannam	/kwan/
			barbam	/bwarba/	sanguis	/swank/
			pascuam	/pwask/	largum	/lwarga/
/ĕ/	fr	/i/	bene	/bin/	petram	/pitra/
			decem	/dik/	pecoram	/pira/
			leporem	/lipro/	veneris die	/vindre/
			venit	/vin/	integrum	/intrik/
	bl	/ja/	bellum	/bjal/	festam	/fjasta/
			pectinem	/pjakno/	terram	/tjara/
			centum	/čant/	dentem	/djant/
			ferrum	/fjar/		
/ē/	/fr/	/aj/	acetum	/akajt/	mensem	/majs/
			velum	/vajla/	venam	/vajna/
			plenum	/plajn/	monetam	/monajta/
	bl	/a/	stellam	/stala/	teg(u)lam	/takla/
			crescere	/kraskro/	tres	/tra/
			directum	/drat/		
/ĭ/	fr	/aj/	fidem	/fajd/	camisiam	/kamajsa/
					sitim	/sajt/
	bl	/a/	piscem	/pask/	de intro	/drante/
			expingere	/spangro/	firmum	/farm/
			strictum	/strat/	dictum	/dat/
			singulum	/sanglo/	basil(i)cam	/basalka/
			auric(u)lam	/orakla/		
/ī/	fr	/aj/	amicum	/amajk/	ripam	/rajpa/
			farinam	/farajna/	diem	/daj/
			nidum	/najd/	pilam	/pajl/
			finem	/fajn/		
	bl	/e/	mille	/mel/	dicere	/dekro/
			quinque	/čenk/		

B. *Unstressed vowels.*

/a/   /a/ in all positions:

avarosum	/avaraws/	acetum	/akajt/
ardere	/ardar/	radicam	/radajka/
catenam	/katajna/	gannire	/ganer/

/i/, /u/   /e/, /o/, or lacking, depending on position:

frigere	/fregur/	mutandis	/modunde/
gyrare	/ẓerwar/	mugit	/mokua/

All other Lat. unstressed vowels have extremely complex reflexes in Vegl., depending on position in the word and type of syllable. For further details, consult Bartoli, II, 343-349.

C. *Diphthongs.*

C.L.   MOD.   VEGL.

/aw/   fr   /aw/

pauper	/pawper/	causam	/kawsa/
caudam	/kawda/	caulem	/kawl/

   bl   No satisfactory examples.

/ae/   fr   /i/   caelum   /čil/

   bl   /ja/   praesto   /prjast/

/oe/   uncertain   foetit   /fit/

II. Consonants.

A. *Simple consonants.*

1. Initial. Consonants in initial position are normally the same in C.L. and Vegl.:

petram	/pitra/	borea	/bur/
tegulam	/takla/	dentem	/djant/
ceram	/kajra/	gulam	/gawla/
mortem	/mwart/	ripam	/rajpa/

2. Medial. Consonants in medial position are normally the same in C.L. and Mod. Vegl.:

apem	/jupa/	udatum	/dut/
foetit	/fit/	Augustus	/agwast/
pacare	/pakur/	uvam	/jojva/
filam	/fajla/	peram	/pajra/

3. Palatalization, however, is normal for velar consonants in both initial and medial positions before Lat. /i/ end /ɛ/, but not before Lat. /e/:

centum	/čant/	reginam	/reğajna/
certum	/čart/	gentem	/ʒjant/
cimicem	/činko/	argentum	/arʒjant/

decem	/dikʈ	gelatum	/gelut/
ceram	/kajra/	ungere	/jongar/
acetum	/akajt/	expingere	/spangro/

Palatalization also appears to be normal for velar consonants before reflexes of Lat. /ū/:

| siccu + -uram | /sečojra/ | culum | /čol/ |
| nec + -unum | /nenčojn/ | obscurum | /sčor/ |

4. Final: Latin final consonants are lacking in Vegl.:

| tres | /tra/ | placet | /pluk/ |

B. *Consonant clusters.*

1. Geminate consonants are everywhere simplified in Mod. Vegl.:

sellam	/sjala/	terram	/tjara/
buccam	/bwak/	ossum	/vwas/
missam	/masa/	ferrum	/fjar/

2. Consonant plus Lat. /j/ usually shows palatalized results in Mod. Vegl.:

| filium | /fel'/ | rationem | /rasawn/ |
| oleum | /vwal'/ | glacies | /glaz/ |

3. Consonant plus /w/: The labial element was lost early before front vowels, permitting palatalization:

coquinam	/kučajna/	anguillam	/anğola/
quinque	/čenk/	conquaerendum	/končaran/

Examples before back vowels are scarce, but seem to indicate loss of labial element:

cuando	/kun/
qualis	/kul/
quadriale	/kadrjal/

4. Consonant plus /l/: These groups normally remain intact in Mod. Vegl.:

clavem	/kluf/	duplum	/duplir/
plenum	/plajn/	oculum	/vaklo/
flumen	/flojm/		

5. Consonant plus /t/ or /s/: The data show /t/ as the Mod. Vegl. reflex of Lat. /kt/, /pt/ for /pt/, with few examples for /ks/ or /ps/:

lectum	/l'at/	septem	/sjapto/
pectus	/pjat/	neptam	/n'apta/
aspectam	/aspjata/		
strictum	/strat/		
noctem	/nwat/	kapsam	/kwas/
exsuctum	/sot/		
dictum	/dat/		

Appendix C

CHART OF THE VOWEL HISTORY OF VEGLIOTE, SERBO-CROATIAN, AND VENETIAN

PERIOD ONE (VEGL. LAT.)																					
Type of syllable	blocked	free	free	blocked	blocked	free	free	blocked	blocked	free	free	blocked	blocked	free	
Phonemes	i		e		ɛ		a		ɔ		o		u		
Phonetic values	i	i:	e:j	e	jɛ	jɛ:	a:	a	wɔ	wɔ:	o:w	o	u	u:	I

free   blocked (from a)

PERIOD TWO

Phonemes	i	i:	e:	e	ɛ	ɛ:	ɔ:	ɔ	o:	o	u	u:	
Phonetic values	i	i:	e:j	e	jɛ	jɛ:	wɔ:	wɔ	o:w	o	u	u:	III

PERIOD THREE

Phonemes	i	ij	ej	e	jɛ	iɛ	u̯ɔ	wɔ	ow	o	ü	üj	Va
Phonemes	i		e		iɛ		ü	u̯ɔ		o		o	Vb

PERIOD FOUR (MOD. VEGL.)

| Phonemes | i | | e | | a | | o | | u | VIII |

MOD. VEGL. EQUIVALENTS OF VEGL. LAT. VOWELS	blocked	free	free	blocked	blocked	free	free	blocked	blocked	free	free	blocked	blocked	free
	i		e		ɛ		a		ɔ		o		u	
	e	aj	aj	a	ja	i	u	wa	wa	u	aw	u	o	oj

Read the chart as follows:

System I, influenced by II, > III.
System III, influenced by the changes which produced IV, > V.
System V, influenced by VII, and by the changes which produced VI, > VIII.

Schemas VIII, IX, and X represent the respective modern vowel systems.

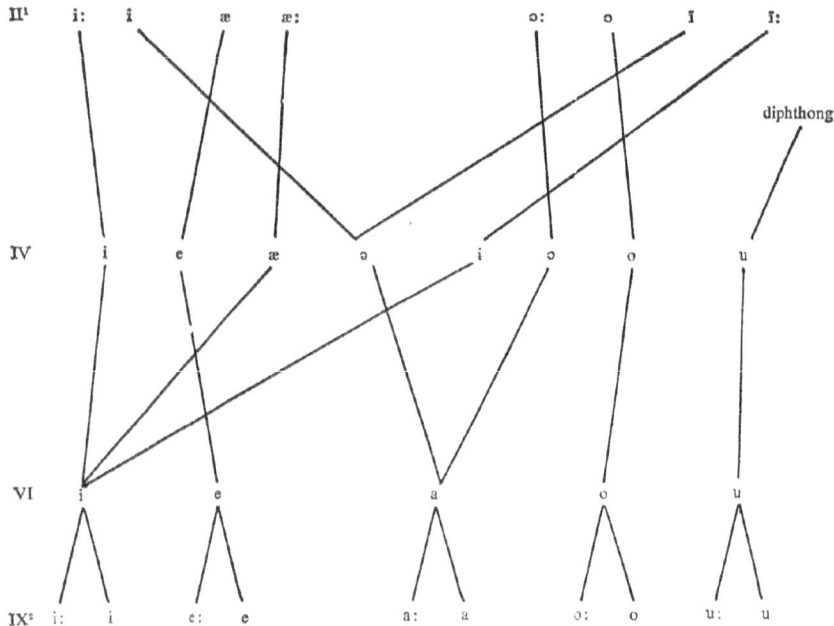

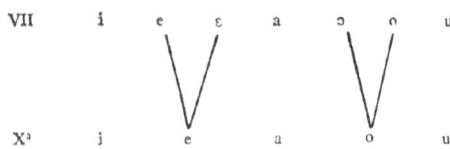

[1] This system is essentially that given by Mareš (1956, 445). I have used different symbols to make the relation of SCr. and Vegl. Lat. phonemes more apparent.
[2] /r/ is omitted from this schema because there is disagreement among Slavicists as to whether [r] represents a separate vowel phoneme, or is to be analyzed as /ə/ + /r/. In either case, it does not affect the history of Vegl.
[3] The reduction to a five-vowel system has not taken place in all areas where Ven. is spoken.

A full-size version of this chart is available to view at:
https://www.uncpress.org/hadlich_insert_p77-78/

APPENDIX D

DISCUSSION OF SELECTED PROBLEMS

As a result of the non-structural treatment of the Vegl. data by Bartoli, a number of misconceptions have been prevalent about certain details of the history of Vegl. A discussion of some of them is presented here as an appendix since their inclusion throughout the text would have made the description more difficult to follow.

1. C.L. /a/.

The Mod. Vegl. free position equivalent of C.L. stressed /a/ is normally cited as *uo* and *u*.[1] The use of *uo* is misleading first because it misrepresents as a diphthong a sound which Bartoli clearly described as monophthongal ("Einvokalisch": He used the graph $\widehat{u o}$ to represent it). The sound in question has a high back articulation very close to that of [u]. Most important, as has been shown in the phonemic analysis of Appendix A, the sound represented by Bartoli's graph $\widehat{u o}$ is a freely varying allophone of the Mod. Vegl. phoneme /u/.

The Mod. Vegl. equivalent of C.L. stressed /a/ in free syllable should be cited as /u/, since failure to do so obscures the fact that the phonemic results of Lat. /a/ and /ɔ/ are identical in Mod. Vegl., that a merger of these phonemes had occurred, and that this merger almost certainly took place before the development of vowel differentiation.[2]

---

[1] E.g., LAUSBERG, 1956, I, 163; TAGLIAVINI, 1948, 264; BOURCIEZ, 1946, 152; MEYER-LÜBKE, 1935, 8596.

[2] If the merger were not pre-vowel-differentiation, it would be difficult to explain why Mod. Vegl. maintains the *Latin* syllable pattern. I.e., Lat.

2. C.L. /a/, /ĕ/, and /ŏ/.

The development of the Vegl. vowel system has been treated in several articles by Petar Guberina.[3] Although Dr. Guberina uses an essentially non-structural approach, the conclusions reached in the present work are essentially in agreement with his findings, at least as to the relatively early development of diphthongs for Lat. /i/, /e/, /o/, and /u/ in free syllable, and the early development of /ɛ/ > /i/ and /a/, /ɔ/ > /u/ in free syllable. Prof. Guberina has proposed, however, that the blocked syllable diphthongization of Lat. /a/, /ɛ/, and /ɔ/ is a product of the latest period of development in Vegl., brought about by the external influence of a similar blocked syllable diphthongization in Čakavian SCr. of northern Yugoslavia.

The information presented by Guberina is well organized and on the whole convincing. I have persisted in suggesting that diphthongization of /ɛ/, /ɔ/, and /a/ was a characteristic of the earliest period of the history of Vegl. (harking back to Vegl. Lat.) because to my mind this is more consistent with all of the facts. Below are some examples of historical problems which prevent me from accepting without question Guberina's suggestion of late development.

a. The diphthong being discussed does not affect Mod. Vegl. /a/, as Guberina suggests, but rather the reflexes of Lat. /a/. Mod. Vegl. /a/ from other sources is not affected.

Consider the following examples:

LAT.	MOD. VEGL.	VARIANTS FOUND IN THE DATA [4]
directum	/drat/	none
firmum	/farm/	fiarm, fierm
argentum	/arǧant/	arjant, arẓant
crescere	/kraskro/	crascere, kresur

/a/ and /ɔ/ show the same results in what had been Lat. free syllable (/u/) and the same results in what had been Lat. blocked syllable (/wa/).

[3] 1955-56, 1960.

[4] As has been discussed (above, 71), non-Vegl. variants were frequently perpetrated by the informant, due to his imperfect knowledge of the language. All variants are offeredhere to show that no diphthong of the type [wo], [wa], imputed by GUBERINA to SCr. influence, is anywhere evident for Mod. Vegl. /a/ in blocked syllable.

LAT.	MOD. VEGL.	VARIANTS FOUND IN THE DATA
singulum	/sanglo/	saingla
de intro	/drante/	none
basilicam	/basalka/	bassalka, bazalka, basaika, bazaika, basalk, bizolk, basaita
cristam	/grasta/	none
piscem	/pask/	pias
expingere	/spangro/	none
fidem	/fajd/	fjad
acetum	/akajt/	acait, acaid, kait
episcopus	/pasku/	none

Compare a few examples from *Latin* /a/, where /u/ or /wa/ are expected in Mod. Vegl.:

cane	/kun/	kuon, cuan
capu	/kup/	cuop
alba	/jwalb/	juolb
larga	/lwarga/	luorga, luarg .
pascua	/pwask/	puoscua, pask, Puosk
pastu	/pwast/	pustuot, putsch
sanguis	/swang/	suank
arbor	/jwarbol/	jarbul, jarbur, garbr, albr, juarbul
canna	/kwan/	none

Since there is no evidence for diphthongization of Mod. Vegl. /a/ from sources other Lat. /a/ and /ɔ/, the necessary conclusion is that the diphthongization took place prior to the development of this modern /a/. Yet this Mod. Vegl. /a/ is attested from the fourteenth century on: E.g., in 1398, *basilica* appears as *Bassalcha*;[5] in 1593 *benedicta* appears as *benedata*,[6] etc.

b. Guberina steadfastly refuses to consider that monophthongal Mod. Vegl. forms /i/ and /u/ for Lat. /ɔ/ and /ɔ/ in free syllable may ever have had a dipthongal shape, even though simplification of diphthongs is widespread in the history of the Romance lan-

---

[5] SKOK, 1927, 98.
[6] *Ibid.*, 97.

guages. The very development /ɛ/ > /jɛ/ > /i/ is in fact found in areas of northern Italy under very similar structural conditions.[7]

Refusal to accept the possibility of an earlier diphthongal shape for Mod. Vegl. /i/ (< Lat. /ɛ/) causes grave difficulties in accounting for the apparent paradox of the Vegl. vowel shifts /i/ > /e/ and /ɛ/ > /i/.

Finally Guberina chooses to ignore the relation to Vegl. of the RRom. dialects which, at an early stage, showed so many points in common with it (e.g. free syllable diphthongization of Lat. /i/, /e/, /o/, and /u/; maintenance of Lat. /aw/; umlaut of stressed /a/ before /-i/; etc.). In these dialects, once spoken in an area very close to Veglia, as well as in areas of No. Italy and Switzerland where no Slavic influence is possible, one finds diphthongization of Lat. /ɛ/ and /ɔ/ in *both* free and blocked syllable. It is unreasonable, in the face of vowel developments parallel at so many points between RRom. and Vegl., to deny the possibility of parallelism cn the diphthongization of Lat. /ɛ/ and /ɔ/ in free syllable at an early stage.

c. A case can be made that diphthongization of Lat /ɛ/ and /ɔ/ took place before the simplification of geminate consonants, based on development of the type Lat. /terra/ > Mod. Vegl. /tjara/, /sella/ > /sjala/. If words of this type had not diphthongized before the simplification of geminates, they would not show the blocked syllable development, since their Mod. Vegl. form has a free stressed syllable. Unfortunately, the majority of the modern data permit of both Guberina's and my interpretations on this point, since Lat. words of the type /collu/ (Mod. Vegl. /kwal/) and /dossu/ (Mod. Vegl. /dwas/) appear in blocked syllable both in Mod. Vegl. and in Vegl. Lat.

d. Although I cannot accept at this point Guberina's contention that there was no early diphthongization of Lat. /a/, /ɔ/ and /ɛ/, it seems to me quite possible that modern SCr. diphthongal developments for low vowels could have had a strong effect on Mod. Vegl. The confusion of native Vegl. /wa/ with SCr. [uo], for example, by bilingual speakers (and indeed in the speech of the last speaker of Vegl.) could account for much of the great variety of forms that are found in the Mod. Vegl. data.

---

[7] See above, 48, n. 3.

3. C.L. /ō/ and /ŭ/.

A most notable feature of Bartoli's analysis is the fact that C.L. /ō/ and /ŭ/ in blocked position are indicated to have different equivalents in Mod. Vegl. (/a/ and /u/, respectively). The implication is that C. L. /ō/ and /ŭ/ did not merge in Vegl. Lat. and that there is the possibility that Vegl. is more closely associated with Rum. and Sard. at this point than with any of the West Romance languages, since in Rum. and Sard., C.L. /ŭ/ and /ō/ remain separate, falling together with /ū/ and /ŏ/, respectively. There is in fact no relation with Rum. and Sard. here since C.L. /ŭ/ and /ō/ had merged in all positions in the Latin of Veglia.

a) The Vegl. development of C.L. /ŭ/ is undeniably different from that of Rum. and Sard., since /ŭ/ under no circumstances merges with C.L. /ū/.

b) It is also unquestionable that, as Bartoli indicates, C.L. /ŭ/ and /ō/ merge in Vegl. in free syllable. Both are represented in Mod. Vegl. by /aw/.

c) Bartoli's decision that C. L. /ŭ/ and /ō/ have separate developments is thoroughly supported by the data for /ŭ/ = Mod. Vegl. /u/. However, the equation of C.L. /ō/ with Mod. Vegl. /a/ is based on only two extremely doubtful examples: C. L. *somnium* = Mod. Vegl. /samn/ makes the assumption that the C. L. word contained /ō/, even though C.L. texts and the majority of Romance languages indicate /ŏ/ in this word (e.g. Span. *sueño;* Ital. *sogno*, with open /o/). Further, the SCr. word for "dream" is *san*, which certainly must have effected the Vegl. word. Even Bartoli admits that the second example is odd: Mod. Vegl. /stal/, equivalent to Ital. *stollo*.

There are more examples in the data to establish the relation C.L. /ō/ in blocked syllable = Mod. Vegl. /u/: e.g. *forma* > /furm/; *soricem* > /surko/; etc. This relation is supported by many examples from outside Vegl. For example, in a text from Zara of A.D. 1441, words in C.L. *-ōre, ōne, -ōr(i)a* usually show *-ur, -un,* and *-ura.*[8] In addition, many SCr. loans show both C.L. /ō/ and /ŭ/ as *u*: *nipotem* > SCr. *neput, rationem* > *račun, cipulla,* > *kapula, sulphur* > *sunpor.*[9]

---

[8] BARTOLI, 1906, II, 401.
[9] *Ibid.*, 398.

d) Since it is unquestionable that C.L. /ŭ/ and /ō/ in free syllable have the same reflex in Mod. Vegl. (/aw/), and since probabilities are very great that the reflex in blocked position is also the same for these phonemes, (i.e., /u/), there is no recourse but to assume that C.L. /ŭ/ and /ō/ were represented by one phoneme (/o/) in the Latin of Veglia.

The assumption that Mod. Vegl. /u/ represents an unchanged continuation of Lat. /ŭ/ is incorrect. It was modified in the course of the history of Vegl., and its return to its original shape was merely a fortuitous development, being a function of the peculiarly Vegliote phonological history.

4. The development of the groups /kt/, /ks/, /pt/, and /ps/.

The decision of Bartoli that C. L. /pt/ and /ps/ are maintained in Mod. Vegl. seems fairly well supported by the data. [10] Examples: *septem* > /sjapto/, *nepta* > /n'apta/.

There are no clear examples for the development of C. L. /ks/.

The development of the group /kt/ has come under considerable discussion since the publication of Bartoli's work on Dalmatian. Opinions have varied greatly on the correct analysis of the results. Bartoli offers evidence of three different results in Mod. Vegl.: (a) /kt/ > /pt/ (*octem* > /wapto/); (b) /kt/ > /jt/ (*factum* > /fajt/); and (c) preservation of /kt/ (*pectinem* > /pjakno/ [*sic*]). [11] In his review of *Das Dalmatische,* Merlo correctly pointed out the inaccuracy of Bartoli's description. [12]

a) /kt/ > /pt/ is completely unacceptable since it is based primarily on one example (/wapto/ = 'otto'), which shows a probable analogical formation based on /sjapto/ = 'sette'. Even Bartoli finally admitted in 1926 that /pt/ was not a Mod. Vegl. development for C.L. /kt/.

b) There are only two examples for the relation /kt/ > /jt/: *factum* > /fajt/ and *fructum* > /frojt/. The former is a poor example, since it also appears in the data as /fwat/, which shows normal vowel development for /a/. Perhaps more important, in II, 481, Bartoli points out that the extension of the past participle ending in *-itus* (> -/ajt/) is quite frequent, making such an analogical exten-

---

[10] BARTOLI, 1906, II, 401.
[11] *Ibid.,* 398.
[12] MERLO, 1907.

sion probable for /fajt/. /frojt/ has the disadvantage that /oj/ is a normal result of /ū/, and it cannot be determined with certainty whether the /j/ is from /ū/, or from /kt/.

c) For the preservation of /kt/, /pjakno/ is the example offered by Bartoli, and it does not contain /kt/. This example can serve only as evidence that the group /kt/ was still intact at the time that *pectine* lost its unaccented *i*. Even this by no means certain (cf. *vetulum* > *veclu*).

Merlo's most strenuous objection is that Bartoli chooses to reject as abnormal a large number of frequently occurring items showing that /kt/ > Mod. Vegl. /t/. [13] Some examples:

lectu	/l'at/	nocte	/nwat/
pectu	/pjat/	exsuctu	/sot/
aspecta	/aspjata/	dictu	/dat/
strictu	/strat/		

Merlo's position is that /t/ is the normal result of /kt/ in Mod. Vegl. He is supported in this opinion by Meyer-Lübke, who maintains, however, that this result is due to the influence of Ven. [14]

Skok has offered evidence from SCr. loans that /ks/ and /kt/ were maintained in Old Dalmatian, and that any later SCr. change to /jt/ is due to a spreading of West Romance tendencies, or to the influence of the Greek spirantization of pre-consonantal velar stops (e.g. [ktenion] > [xteni]). [15]

The Old Vegl. preservation of /kt/ (along with /ks/, /pt/, and /ps/) seems the best interpretation, with the simplification to /t/ attributable to later Ven. influence.

5. East or West?

In his analysis, Bartoli reached the conclusion that Vegl. is a member of the Appenino-Balkan (or East) Romance language group. The structural analysis of the history of Vegl. shows that this conclusion is not completely accurate. The following is a discussion of major criteria used to establish a position of Vegl. among the Romance languages.

---

[13] MERLO, 1907, 275.
[14] MEYER-LÜBBKE, 1925, 19.
[15] SKOK, 1934, 427.

a) Vowels.

As has been shown (above, 83-84), the fact that C.L. /ŭ/ is represented by /u/ in Mod. Vegl. cannot be used to liken Vegl. to Rum., since the structural development of C.L. /ŭ/ in Vegl. is completely different from that in Rum. Since C.L. /ŭ/ and /ō/ were represented by one phoneme, /o/, in the Latin of Veglia, the vowel system by the beginning of the seventh century was the same as that postulated for the early period of all of the West Romance languages (see Appendix C, I), and is distinctly to be contrasted to the East group. Furthermore, the phonetic values of the Vegl. Lat. vowels show allophonic patterning which was characteristic of many areas of the West (e.g. Raetia, areas of No. Italy, France), but not of the East.

Certain vowel changes subsequent to the beginning of PSCr. influence also should be considered essentially Western developments. Although the simplification of Latin long consonants is unrelated to the similar Western development (see below, 87) the manner in which the Vegl. system adjusted to this externally induced change follows a distinctly western pattern: the differentiation of Vegl. vowels, and the ultimate phonemicization of /j/ and /w/ follows the same structural process in Vegl., RRom., and French. In Rum., on the other hand, when long consonants are simplified, the system does not adjust by means of vowel differentiation because its vowel system, due to the great distance of Dacia from Northern Italy, did not have the Western characteristic of long vowels in free syllable necessary for the differentiation of vowels. [16]

---

[16] It is suggested that the impending loss of the systemic redundancy offered by the contrast long:short in the Rum. consonant system was a primary factor in the development of a qualitative contrast in the liquids and nasals, a development lacking in Vegl., where vowel differentiation was the result of loss of consonant length: Lat. -ll- > Rum. /l/, or /ø/, depending on the adjacent vowels, but Lat. -l- > Rum. /r/: callem > /cale/, stella > /steə/, but talem > /tare/. In the case of /nn/:/n/, the feature of length was replaced by a qualitative change in the contiguous vowels: Lat. -nn- simplifies and produces no change in vowels, but Lat. -n- produces the change /a/ > /ï/: Lat. annum > Rum. /an/, but anum > /ïn/.

It has been further pointed out that there is a relation between the development of quantitative distinctions between /ll/:/l/, /nn/:/n/, and the lack of vowel differentiation in Rum., Ibero-Romance, and dialects of

Thus, if a division of Romance languages were to be made on the basis of vowel development, Vegl. would have to be considered a West Romance language.

b) Consonants.

Consideration of the development of the Vegl. consonant system leads one to the exactly opposite conclusion: that Vegl. is an East Romance language.

1) The Vegl. preservation of Lat. groups /kt/, /ks/, /pt/, and /ps/ (above, 84-85) is an example of divergence of Vegl. from the West Romance languages, in which some modification (assimilation, palatalization) is normal.

2) Characteristic West Romance lenition of consonants,[17] manifested especially in the sonorization of intervocalic voiceless stops and the spirantization of intervocalic voiced stops, is completely absent in Vegl.

3) The loss of phonemic consonant length in the West is generally considered to be structurally related to the lenitive process just referred to. Although the history of Vegl. apparently displays the same loss of phonemic consonant length, the Vegl. process differs structurally in that long consonants merge with the corresponding short consonants, and in the lack of structurally related lenition of intervocalic voiced and voiceless stops. The loss of phonemic consonant length in Vegl., brought about by the influence of PSCr., must be considered a non-Western development.

4) The contrast between Vegl. and West Romance palatalization of /k/ and /g/ before front vowels goes deeper than the apparent Vegl. lack of palatalization before /e/ (i.e., /ki/ > /čaj/, but /ke/ > /kaj/).[18] A further difference is the fact that, in West Romance, the results of Lat. /k/ and /g/ before /i/ and /e/ are normally the same as for /k/ and /g/ before Lat. /j/ (e.g. *cinctura* > French /sætür/; *centum* > French /sã/; *glacies* > French /glas/), while in Vegl., as in Rum., these two groups are kept separate (/ki/ > /č/; /kj/ > /ɛ/; etc.).[19] The most important

---

Southern France: Haudricourt—Juilland, 1949, 52; and Weinrich, 1958, 183-188.

[17] MARTINET, 1952.

[18] I.e., palatalization takes place before *Vegl.* /e/ (=C.L. /ī/) but not before *Vegl.* /a/ (=C.L. /ē/).

[19] Haudricourt—Juilland, 1949, 80.

difference between Vegl. and the West, however, resides in the structural factors underlying the development of palatal phonemes (discussed on pages 53-54, above). This basic difference in the phonological development in Vegl. and in the West forces the decision that also at this point in the development of consonants, Vegl. is clearly *not* a West Romance language.

c) Thus the Vegl. vowel system developed like those of the West Romance languages and the consonant system developed like those of the East Romance languages. This situation resulted from the chronology of the changes which characterize the West Romance languages. That is, the changes characteristic of the West Romance vowel systems had already taken place (including in Vegl. Lat.) by the time that Veglia was isolated from the West by the Slavs. However, the Western consonant changes took place considerably after this isolation, so that West Romance influence on changes in Veglia was impossible.

We must revise Bartoli's placing of Vegl. in the East Romance group, and consider Vegl. rather a linguistic system in which, according to the normal criteria, the East-West division of Romance languages does not apply.

BIBLIOGRAPHY

BIBLIOGRAPHICAL ABBREVIATIONS

AGI	Archivio glottologico italiano.
ASNS	Archiv für das Studium der neueren Sprachen.
AT	Annali delle università toscane.
BSDI	Bullettino della Società Dantesca Italiana.
BZRP	Beihefte zur Zeitschrift für romanische Philologie.
CSP	Cahiers Sextil Puşcariu.
DLZ	Deutsche Literatur-Zeitung.
ID	Italia dialettale.
IJ	Indogermanisches Jahrbuch.
LGRP	Literaturblatt für germanische und romanische Philologie.
PMLA	Publications of the Modern Language Association of America.
RDR	Revue de dialectologie romane.
RF	Romanische Forschungen.
RFIC	Rivista de filologia e istruzione classica.
RIL	Rendiconti del Reale Istituto Lombardo de Scienze e Lettere.
RLR	Revue de linguistique romane.
RP	Romance Philology.
SR	The Slavonic and East Europe Review.
SRAZ	Studia romanica et anglica Zagrabiensia.
TCLP	Travaux du Cercle Linguistique de Prague.
ZRP	Zeitschrift für romanische Philologie.
ZSP	Zeitschrift für slavische Philologie.

BIBLIOGRAPHY

ALARCOS LLORACH, EMILIO. *Fonología española*. 2nd ed. Madrid, 1954.
ASCOLI, GRAZIADIO I. Saggi ladini, *AGI* 1, 1873, 1-556.
———. Piccolo contributo allo studio del veglioto, *AGI* 20, 1926, 127-131.
BARIĆ, H. *O uzajamnim odnosima balkanskih jezika*. I. Ilirskoromanska jezička grupa. Belgrad, 1937. (Summary by N. Jokl in *IJ* 24, 1940, 229-231.)
BARTOLI, MATTEO G. *Das Dalmatische:* altromanische Sprachreste von Veglia bis Ragusa und ihre Stellung in der appeninobalkanischen Romania. Schriften der Balkankommission, Vols. 4, 5. Vienna, 1906.
———. Note dalmatiche, *ZRP* 32, 1907, 1-16.
———. Riflessi slavi di vocali labiale romani e romanze, greche, e germaniche, *Festschrift... Ignatii Jagić*, 30-60. Berlin, 1908.
———. Dalmazia e Albania. Relazione sul Quinquennio 1905-1910, *RDR* 2, 1910, 456-490.
———. Ancora Veglia ed aree vicine, *AGI* 20, 1926, 132-139.
BESZARD, LUCIEN. Review of Bartoli, 1906, *Nyelvtudomanyi* 32, 1908, 122-123.
BIDWELL, CHARLES E. The chronology of certain sound changes in Common Slavic as evidenced by loans from Vulgar Latin, *Word* 17, 1961, 105-127.
BLOOMFIELD, LEONARD. *Language*. New York, 1933.
BOERIO, GIUSEPPE. *Dizionario del dialetto veneziano*. 3rd ed., Venice, 1867.
BONFANTE, GIULIANO. A remark on phonologic change, *PMLA* 61, 1946, 1-6.
BOURCIEZ, EDOUARD. *Eléments de linguistique romane*. 4th ed. Paris, 1946.
BROWN, HORATIO. R. F. *The Venetian Republic*. London, 1902.
COSERIU, EUGENIO. *Sincronía, diacronía, e historia:* el problema del cambio lingüístico. Montevideo, 1958.
DEVOTO, GIACOMO. Per la storia della latinità euganea. I. Il gruppo *kl*, *Melanges... Michaelson*, 66-97. Gøteborg, 1952.
ELMENDORF, JOHN V. *An etymological dictionary of the Dalmatian dialect of Veglia*. Unpublished doctoral dissertation, University of No. Carolina. Chapel Hill, 1951.
GARTNER, THEODOR. Review of Bartoli, 1906, *ZRP* 31, 1907, 619-621.
———. *Handbuch der rätoromanischen Sprache und Literatur*. Halle, 1910.
GUBERINA, PETAR. L'état du vocalisme dans le vegliote moyen et moderne, *Annales de l'Institut Français de Zagreb* 4-5, 1955-56, 23-28.
———. La diphtongaison vegliote est-elle une diphtongaison romane? Congresso internazionale di studi romanzi, 8th, Florence, 1956; *Atti*, Vol. II, pt. 2-3, 537-548. Florence, 1960.

GUBERINA, PETAR. Le problème de la diphtongaison en vegliote, *SRAZ* 9-10, 1960, 137-148.
HALL, ROBERT A., Jr., The reconstruction of Proto-Romance, *Language* 26, 1950, 6-27.
HAUDRICOURT, ANDRÉ G. AND JUILLAND, ALPHONSE G. *Essai pour une histoire structurale du phonétisme français.* Paris, 1949.
———. Romania orientale et Romania occidentale dans le vocalisme, *CSP* 1, 1952, 241-254.
HODGE, CARLTON T. Serbo-Croatian phonemes, *Language* 22, 1946, 112-120.
IVIĆ, PAVLE. *Die serbokroatischen Dialekte.* The Hague, 1958.
HOENIGSWALD, HENRY M. *Language change and linguistic reconstruction.* Chicago, 1960.
JACKSON, T. G. *Dalmatia, the Quarnero, and Istria.* 3 Vols. Oxford, 1887.
JUD, JACOB. Review of Bartoli, 1906, *ASNS* 121, 1909, 425-435.
JUD, JACOB, AND JABERG, KARL. *Sprach- und Sachatlas Italiens und der Südschweiz.* Zofingen, 1928-1940.
JIRIČEK, KONSTANTIN. Die Romanen in den Städten Dalmatiens während des Mittelalters, *Denkschriften der kaiserlichen Akademie der Wissenschaften,* Philosophisch-Historische Klasse, 48, 1902, 63-78, and 49, 1903, 1-72.
JUILLAND, ALPHONSE G. A bibliography of diachronic phonemics, *Word* 9, 1953, 198-208.
KUHN, ALWIN. *Romanische Philologie.* Bern, 1951.
LAUSBERG, HEINRICH. *Die Mundarten Südlukaniens.* Halle, 1939.
———. Zum romanischen Vokalismus, *RF* 60, 1947, 295-307.
———. *Romanische Sprachwissenschaft.* 2 vols. Berlin, 1956.
LESKIEN, AUGUST. *Grammatik der serbokroatischen Sprache.* Heidelberg, 1914.
LÜDTKE, HELMUT. *Die strukturelle Entwicklung des romanischen Vokalismus.* Bonn, 1956.
LUNT, HORACE G. *Old Church Slavonic Grammar.* 2nd ed. The Hague, 1959.
MAREŠ, FRANTIŠEK V. L'Origine du système phonologique slave et son évolution jusqu'au bout de l'époque de l'unité linguistique slave, *Slavia* 25, 1956, 443-495.
MARTINET, ANDRÉ. Rôle de la correlation dans la phonologie diachronique, *TCLP* 8, 1939, 273-288.
———. Function, structure and sound change, *Word* 8, 1952, 1-32.
———. Diffusion of language and structural linguistics, *RP* 6, 1952, 5-13.
———. Celtic lenition and Western Romance consonants, *Language* 28, 1952, 192-217.
———. *Economie des changements phonétiques.* Traité de phonologie diachronique. Berne, 1955.
MEILLET, ANTOINE. *Le slave commun.* Paris, 1934.
MEILLET, ANTOINE AND VAILLANT, ANDRÉ. *Grammaire de la langue serbo-croate.* 2nd. ed. Paris, 1952.
MENÉNDEZ PIDAL, RAMÓN. *Manual de gramática histórica española.* 9th ed. Madrid, 1952.
MERLO, CLEMENTE. Dalmatico e latino a proposito di una pubblicazione recente, *RFIC* 35, 1907, 472-484.
———. Ancora del dalmatico, *AT* 30, 1910, 1-24.
———. Veglioto e ladino, *RIL* 43, 1910, 271-281.
———. L'Italia dialettale, *ID* 1, 1924, 12-26.

MERLO, CLEMENTE. Edito's note to Battisti, Bullettino bibliografico, *ID* 5, 1929, 285-289, n. 2.
———. Veglioto e ladino, *Ce fastu?* 30, 1954, 36-42.
MEYER-LÜBKE, WILHELM. *Historische Grammatik der französchen Sprache.* Berlin, 1908.
———. Rumänisch, Romanisch, und Albanesisch, *Mitteilungen des rumänischen Instituts an der Univ. Wien* 1, 1914, 1-44.
———. Beiträge zur romanischen Laut- und Formenlehre, *ZRP* 45, 1925, 641-663.
———. *Romanisches etymologisches Wörterbuch.* Heidelberg, 1935.
NOVAK, VIKTOR. The Slavonic-Latin symbiosis in Dalmatia during the middle ages. *SR* 32, 1953, 1-28.
PARODI, ERNESTO. Review of Bartoli, 1906, *BSDI* 14, 1907, 149-150.
PENZL, HERBERT. The evidence for phonemic changes, *Studies... Whatmough.* 193-208. The Hague, 1957.
PETROVICI, EMIL. Kann das Phonemsystem einer Sprache durch fremden Einfluss umgestaltet werden? Zum slavischen Einfluss auf das rumänische Lautsystem. *Janua Linguarum* 3, The Hague, 1957.
POLITZER, FRIEDA N., AND POLITZER, ROBERT, L. *Romance trends in 7th and 8th century Latin documents.* Chapel Hill, 1953.
POLITZER, ROBERT L. A note on North Italian voicing of intervocalic stops, *Word* 11, 1955, 416-419.
POPOVIĆ, IVAN. *Geschichte der serbokroatischen Sprache.* Wiesbaden, 1960.
PULGRAM, ERNST. *The tongues of Italy: prehistory and history.* Cambridge (Mass.), 1958.
———. On prehistoric linguistic expansion, *For Roman Jakobson,* 411-417. The Hague, 1956.
PUŞCARIU, SEXTIL. Review of Bartoli, 1906, *DLZ* 28, 1907, 2501-506.
REICHENKRON, GÜNTER. *Beiträge zur romanischen Lautlehre.* Jena and Leipzig, 1939.
———. Einige methodische Bemerkungen zur serbokroatisch-romanischen Wortgleichung, *ZSP* 25, 1956, 163-175.
RICHTER, ELISE. *Beiträge zur Geschichte der Romanismen:* I. Chronologische Phonetik des Französischen bis zum Ende des 8 Jahrhundert. *BZRP* 82, 1934.
ROHLFS, GERHARD. *Historische Grammatik der italienischen Sprache.* 3 vols. Berne, 1949.
ROSAMANI, ENRICO. *Vocabolario giuliano.* Bologna, 1958.
ROSENKRANZ, BERNHARD. Die Gliederung des Dalmatischen, *ZRP* 71, 1955, 269-279.
SCHÜRR, FRIEDRICH. La posizione storica del romagnolo fra i dialetti contermini, *RDR* 9, 1933, 203-228.
———. Umlaut und Diphthongierung, *RF* 50, 1936, 275-316.
———. La diphtongaison romane, *RLR* 20, 1956, 107-144.
SKOK, PETER. Studi toponomastici sull'isola de Veglia, *AGI* 21, 1927, 95-106; 24, 1930, 19-55; 25, 1931, 117-137; 28, 1936, 54-63; 29, 1937, 113-119.
———. Einiges Neue aus dem Altdalmatischen und dem Serbo-Kroatischen, *ZRP* 57, 1937, 462-480.
———. O zamjeni vl. $\bar{u} >$ sl. *y, Časopis za slovenski jezik* 6, 1927, 1-7.
———. Zur Chronologie der Palatalisierung von *k, g, kw, gw* vor *e, i,* und *i̯* im Balkanlatein, *ZRP* 46, 1926, 385-410.

SKOK, PETER. Zum Balkanlatein, *ZRP* 48, 1928, 398-403; 50, 1930, 484-532; 54, 1934, 424-499.

———. La diphtongue latine *au* dans les langues balkaniques, *Mélanges... Roques* 4, 1952, 241-249.

STRAKA, GEORGES. La dislocation linguistique de la Romania et la formation des langues romanes à la lumière de la chronologie relative des changements phonetiques, *RLR* 20, 1956, 249-267.

SWADESH, MORRIS. Observation of pattern impact on the phonetics of bilinguals, *Language, Culture, and Personality*, 59-65. Menasha (Wisc.), 1941.

TAGLIAVINI, CARLO. *Le origini delle lingue neolatine*. Bologna, 1948.

TAMARO, ATTILIO. *La Vénétie Julienne et la Dalmatie*. 3 vols. Rome, 1918-19.

TOGEBY, KNUD. Les explications phonologiques historiques sont-elles possibles? *RP* 13, 1960, 401-413.

VIDOS, B. E. *Manuale di linguistica romanza*. Florence, 1959.

WARTBURG, WALTHER VON. *Die Ausgliederung der romanischen Sprachräume*. Berne, 1950.

WEINREICH, URIEL. *Languages in contact*. New York, 1953.

WEINRICH, HARALD. *Phonologische Studien zur romanischen Sprachgeschichte*. Münster-Westfalen, 1958.

ZAUNER, ADOLF. Review of Bartoli, 1906, *LGRP* 24, 1907, 122-124.

www.ingramcontent.com/pod-product-compliance
Lightning Source LLC
Chambersburg PA
CBHW020422230426
43663CB00007BA/1268